Dog Years

Mark Doty's seven books of poetry and three books of non-fiction prose have been honoured with such distinctions as the T. S. Eliot Prize, the National Book Critics Circle Award, the PEN / Martha Albrand Award, the Los Angeles Times Book Prize and a fellowship from the Guggenheim Foundation. He is a professor at the University of Houston and lives in New York City.

Dog Years

a memoir

Mark Doty

Jonathan Cape
London

Published by Jonathan Cape 2008

2 4 6 8 10 9 7 5 3 1

First published in Great Britain in 2008 by
Jonathan Cape
Random House, 20 Vauxhall Bridge Road,
London SW1V 2SA

www.rbooks.co.uk

Addresses for companies within The Random House Group Limited can be found at:
www.randomhouse.co.uk

The Random House Group Limited Reg. No. 954009

A CIP catalogue record for this book is available from the British Library

ISBN 9780224080910

The Random House Group Limited supports The Forest Stewardship
Council (FSC), the leading international forest certification organisation.
All our titles that are printed on Greenpeace approved FSC certified paper carry the FSC logo.
Our paper procurement policy can be found at
www.rbooks.co.uk/environment

Mixed Sources
Product group from well-managed
forests and other controlled sources
www.fsc.org Cert no. TT-COC-2139
© 1996 Forest Stewardship Council

Printed and bound in Great Britain by
CPI Mackays, Chatham, ME5 8TD

Acknowledgments

The author's deep gratitude to Terry Karten, for good advice, close reading, friendship, and ready help, and to Danny Mulligan and Julia Felsenthal, as well as to the Corporation of Yaddo and the University of Houston. To Carol Muske Dukes and Amy Hempel, readers without peer. And to Paul Lisicky, who is in his way the other author of these pages.

... How could God have created the world if He were already everywhere? One cabbalistic response is to assume that He did so by abandoning a region of Himself.

—DARIAN LEADER,
Stealing the Mona Lisa

If your Nerve, deny you—
Go above your Nerve—

—EMILY DICKINSON

I am not lonely. I am not afraid. I am still yours.

—ROBINSON JEFFERS,
"THE HOUSEDOG'S GRAVE"

Contents

Chapter One

No dog has ever said a word, but that doesn't mean they live outside the world of speech. They listen acutely. They wait to hear a term—*biscuit, walk*—and an inflection they know. What a stream of incomprehensible signs passes over them as they wait, patiently, for one of a few familiar words! Because they do not speak, except in the most limited fashion, we are always trying to figure them out. The expression is telling: to "figure out" is to make figures of speech, to invent metaphors to help us understand the world. To choose to live with a dog is to agree to participate in a long process of interpretation—a mutual agreement, though the human being holds most of the cards.

What the interpreter must do is tell stories—sometimes to the dog in question. Who hasn't heard a dog walker chattering away to her pet, as if she were serving as a kind of linguistic mirror: "You are scared of that police horse," "Lola loves that ball!" Some people speak for their dogs in the first person, as though the dog were ventriloquizing his owner. There's inevitably something embarrassing about this; a kind of silly intimacy that might seem sweet at home becomes a source of eye-rolling discomfort to strangers.

But most stories about dogs are narrated to other people, as we go on articulating the tales of our animals' lives, in order to bring their otherwise incomprehensible experience into the more orderly world of speech. Taking pictures of your pet serves much the same function; it isn't just about memory and the desire to record, but a way to bring something of the inchoate into the world of the represented. This is a part of the pet owner's work. In order to live within the domestic world, the dog must be named, read, and in some way understood.

Of course, listening to stories about other people's pets is perilous, like listening to the recitation of dreams. Such reports may be full of charm for the dreamer, but for the poor listener they're usually fatally dull. The dreamer has no distance from the spell of the dream, and cannot say just how it mattered so, and language mostly fails to capture the deeply interior character of dreams anyway. We listen with an appreciation for the speaker's intent, but without much interest in the actual story.

Love itself is a bit like that: you can describe your beloved until the tongue tires and still, in truth, fail to get at the particular quality that has captured you. We give up, finally, and distill such feelings into single images: the bronzy warmth of one of his glances, or that way of turning the head she has when she's thinking and momentarily stops being aware of other people. That, we tell ourselves, stands for what we love. But it's perfectly clear that such images explain nothing. They serve as signposts for some incommunicable thing. Being in love is our most common version of the unsayable; everyone seems to recognize that you can't experience it from the outside, not quite—you have to feel it from the inside in order to know what it is.

Maybe the experience of loving an animal is actually *more* resistant to language, since animals cannot speak back to us, cannot characterize themselves or correct our assumptions about them. They look at us across a void made of the distance between their lives and our immersion in language. "Not a single one of his myriad sensations," wrote Virginia Woolf of Elizabeth Barrett Browning's cocker spaniel, Flush, "ever submitted itself to the deformity of words."

Maybe they remind us, in this way, of our own origins, when our bodies were not yet assumed into the world of speech. Then we could experience wordlessly, which must at once be a painful thing and a strange joy, a pure kind of engagement that adults never know again. Can it even be called "painful" or a "joy," if the infant who is feeling those things has no terms for them, only the uninterpreted life of emotion and sensation? We suffer a loss, leaving the physical world for the world of words—even though we gain our personhood in the process.

Love for a wordless creature, once it takes hold, is an enchantment, and the enchanted speak, famously, in private mutterings, cryptic riddles, or gibberish. This is why I shouldn't be writing anything to do with the two dogs who have been such presences for sixteen years of my life. How on earth could I stand at the requisite distance to say anything that might matter?

Last month five thousand people died here in New York; the ruins of the towers in which—with which—they fell smolder still. [I wrote these words in October of 2001; the dead had not yet been properly counted; it was impossible to find the bodies, and the lists of the missing were unclear.] *When the wind is right, Chelsea fills with the smell of burning plastic, as if somewhere down in the rubble thou-*

sands and thousands of computers were slowly, poisonously burning, along with fluorescent tubes and industrial carpeting and the atomized pieces of corporate art that lined the reception room walls. My friends in other cities speak about the new war, the roots of this atrocity and its relationship to other atrocities around the globe; they worry over the notion of "evil," whether it's a reality or a concept with no use in the public sphere. I understand that such things matter, but for me they're nothing but air.

I can't stop seeing the whitened boots of the rescue workers trudging back uptown, or sitting beside me on the subway benches. Their battered leather and shoelaces, cuffs and ankles are covered with a thick powder composed of atomized concrete: the pulverized stuff of two hundred floors of offices—desk chairs, files, coffee cups—commingled with the stuff of human bodies reduced to creamy ash. The rubble trucks rumble up Eighth Avenue, uncovered. The white grit blows out in troubled eddies, and snow gusts and coats our faces and hair. Somewhere in that dust are the atoms of Graham, a man I knew a little, and saw last at the end of summer, when he was laughing on the street, his tattooed arms flashing in the sun.

With the world in such a state, isn't it arrogance or blind self-absorption to write about your dogs?

Yes and no. Just as my friends' generalizations about the political situation mean little to me now, because they are abstract, so it is hard to apprehend five thousand deaths; the sheer multiplicity of human lives lost makes the fact of those losses ungraspable. The collective may be almost impossible to apprehend, but the individual loss is vital, irreducible; it has the factual character of a single body, and that body's absence. That is why New York is full of posters, images of the dead, left up, even pasted onto more subway walls and lampposts and mailboxes than before, long after it's possible that anyone living will be *found in the rubble. We need to see the faces, look at them one at a time, and absorb whatever bit of detail we're offered, the characterizing information that begins to form a picture of a life: a scar, a titanium plate mending a broken bone, a birthmark starring a hip. What was hidden, a month ago, is now the displayed marker of individuality. We need them to look at us and make themselves real.*

And every death is like that, isn't it? We use the singular to approach the numberless. The local provides a means to imagine the whole. A student of mine lost his brother a year ago to a drunk driver. After the towers fell, he found himself almost obsessively imagining how it must have been for individuals there: did this one's consciousness end in a shower of rubble, did she remain aware after the fall of a steel beam? When, in the downward flight from the hot windows of the building, did this man cease to feel? This relentless visualizing was a sort of self-torture, but it seemed he couldn't stop. Then he realized that the work he was doing, really, was the imaginative investigation of his brother's death. Was there time for pain, for any understanding of what had taken place, or did awareness end with the sudden obliteration of the oncoming car smashing into the driver's door? It seemed necessary to rehearse these possibilities, to feel one's way through what it might be like to die, and dreadful as the fiery deaths downtown were in themselves, they were also a vehicle through which Gill would learn to picture the end of his brother's life.

I began to do the same thing, imagining Graham's last hours. He waits in line, at Logan, a little sleepy still, not as eager as he might like to be for the flight to L.A.; he's thinking about Tim in Provincetown, whom he won't see now for a few days, maybe he's called and said, Hey, you were still asleep when I left ... He's drinking airport coffee, he's reading the newspaper in a casual, half-attentive way, and then he's moving in line to get his boarding pass scanned, he's on the

Jetway, then he's settling into his seat and listening to the recitation of the flight attendants, which he has, without meaning to, memorized. The question, of course, is when does he know? It's not till after take-off, but it can't be long after, if the plane's going to veer off course south and east to New York. What is the first disruption, when does he understand just how disrupted things really are? When the plane changes pilots, is there a swerve or a dip or nothing at all? And as the speed mounts, as the plane descends, when does he know—does he ever know—where they're headed?

And just a few minutes before, I'm walking on West Sixteenth Street toward the F train, on my way to the library, and on the corner, maybe ten people are standing around, facing south, their necks angled up. What are they looking at? From here, the hole in the north tower is a distinctive, unforgettable shape, something like the outline of an unfamiliar continent in a school geography book. A version of Australia. Except there's nothing inside the territory defined by the border, it's blank inside, though ringed, visible even all the way from Sixteenth Street, by flames.

These deaths aren't commensurate: one twenty-one-year-old man denied the fulfillment and adventure of a life does not equal five thousand selves suddenly snuffed out. My acquaintance—my carpenter's boyfriend—hurtling to his arbitrary, unpredictable, hapless death, caught in the machinations of global capitalism, the aftermath of colonial empires, the rise of fundamentalism, the battles for the power-money elixir of petroleum—that's one singular vanishing. No death equals another, really, not when every life is individuated by circumstance and culture, body and desire, the within and without that make us ourselves. I know it might seem absurd, to place the death of my dog on this page with all these people, vanished parents and children and lovers and friends.

Yet Beau's body was a fact, too, wasn't it? The particular pink ruffle of those gums, turning to black at the jowls, and the long curl of the spotted tongue, a wet pink splashed with inkish spots like blotches of berry juice, and the palate with its fine roof of intricate ridges— those were physical, intimate realities that have been swept away. I can no longer take pleasure in seeing and knowing their presence, their actuality. Someone was here, an intelligence and sensibility, a complex of desires and memories, habits and expectations. Someone with a quality of being exactly this: here I am, myself, all tongue and eyes and golden paws reaching forward into what lies ahead. Golden: for me that's forever his word now, and something about that blond shine is gone from the world forever. And something of it remains absolutely clear to me, the quality of him, the aspect of him most inscribed within me.

You can only understand the world through what's at hand.

Everything else is an idea about reality, a picture or a number, a theory or a description. There's nowhere to begin but here.

A while ago, I had a drink with a new acquaintance, who was taking a little time away from his work and had come to the seashore to write a screenplay. Over a beer, in the way that people offer a topic of conversation in order to know one another better, he asked what I'd like to do if my commitments were all waived, if I suddenly had the freedom to choose whatever. I said I'd buy a place with a barn, in the country, and open a shelter for homeless retrievers.

He looked at me a little incredulously. He seemed to be choosing his words carefully. "I don't know," he said, "when people talk about what they want to do for animals, I always wonder why that compassion isn't offered to other people."

My anger flared, a hot, fierce flush. I said, "You asked me what I wanted to do, not what I thought I *should* do."

He nodded. "Fair enough." But the damage was done, the judgment cast. If I'd been more thoughtful and less offended, I might have said that compassion isn't a limited quality, something we can only possess so much of and which thus must be carefully conserved. I might have said, if I was truly being honest, that I've never known anyone holding this opinion to demonstrate much in the way of empathy with other people anyway; it seems that compassion for animals is an excellent predictor of one's ability to care for one's fellow human beings.

But the plain truth is no one should have to defend what he loves. If I decide to become one of those dotty old people who live alone with six beagles, who on earth is harmed by the extremity of my affections? There is little enough devotion in the world that we should be glad for it in whatever form it appears, and never mock it, or underestimate its depths.

Love, I think, is a gateway to the world, not an escape from it.

※ ※

When my partner Wally died, in 1994, my way of dealing with that unassimilable fact was to write a book about it—books, in truth, since I wrote both a memoir and many poems informed by that reverberant, disordering loss. The response to those books was extraordinary, and heartening, but there are always dissatisfied readers, too, and, of course, it's the negative voice that lodges in the back of my skull like a bad song on the radio you can't shake. A particularly sour British critic's words trot themselves out when the opportunity's ripe. The reviewer called me a "vampire feasting on his lover's body." As if one simply didn't have the right to talk about such misery; shouldn't you, after all, buck up, get on with it? We all have our sufferings, dear, now shut up.

The public revelation of grief is unseemly, an embarrassment of self-involvement. Or at least that's how it seems on the surface. The truth is probably that we want grief to remain invisible because we can't do anything about it, and because it invariably reminds us of the losses we'll all suffer someday, the ineluctable approach of sorrow.

For someone grieving for animals, the problem's compounded.

You can't tell most people about the death of your dog, not quite; there is an expectation that you shouldn't overreact, shouldn't place too much weight on this loss. In the scheme of things, shouldn't this be a smaller matter? _It's just a dog; get another one._

One of the unspoken truths of American life is how deeply people grieve over the animals who live and die with them, how real that emptiness is, how profound the silence is these creatures leave in their wake. Our culture expects us not only to bear these losses alone, but to be ashamed of how deeply we feel them.

The death of a pet is, after all, the first death that most of us know. Not long ago, I visited an old hotel on Block Island, a big, white Victorian perched on grassy slopes above inlets leading to the sea. Walking down toward the cove, I came upon the grave of a golden retriever, made by the children of the family that owned the place. It was ringed in stones, and planted with flowers, and bore a wooden sign painted with the dog's name. I recognized it because, back in the house, I'd seen a photograph of his old, white face. In the backyard, there was an Adirondack chair sitting in the grass, and in the seat, a portrait of the missing fellow, a painting of him asleep on a rug, maybe on one of the hotel's windswept porches. The chair and the painting seemed markers of an absence; the grave was tended, honored; both were markers of memory, gestures intended to resist absence, or rather, more precisely, to conserve it. If Elliot was forgotten, he'd be lost again, wouldn't he? But if his absence remained, if the space where he stood or lay on the rug were given attention—then that's a way of keeping something of the dead with us, even if what is kept is an empty outline.

Such a set of rituals represents education in the work of grieving. Such a loss prefigures the ones to come, and, as a point of origin, reverberates throughout a life. It has always startled me that psychology has placed so much emphasis on children's introduction to the world of sexuality; compelling as such discoveries are, can we truly say they matter more to us than our initial discoveries of limit? The child's apprehension of mortality is a set of initiations, woundings, introductions to the mystery, and animals are very often the objects of these instructions. The little turtle in the grass, the lifeless snake on the path, the toad crushed by a boot heel, the caged bird whose animation has fled with its song—they are more than themselves for us as children; they lead us into the depths of this life.

≋≋

I'm walking Arden, our elderly black retriever, on the street in front of the apartment. Arden's been with me since he was a pup, himself retrieved from an animal shelter in Vermont. The fifteen years of his life represent the story of that decade and a half of mine; he's outlived Wally, and came, after a bit of convincing, to

be totally devoted to Paul, the man in my life now. And he's outlived Beau, with whom he shared house and walks and water bowl
for seven years. He seems to have been old for so long! As he's
gradually hobbled by arthritis and cataracts, as his deafness inten-
sifies, he grows more and more touching in his persistence, his
intent to continue his walks and his descents and panting ascents
of the apartment stairs. Paul says that Arden's like one of those
old men you see every morning on the beach in Miami, the barrel-
chested kind in a tight, black bikini who throws himself into the
water for a swim, no matter what the weather; the colder the water
and the more blustery the day, the more he seems to take a fierce
pride in his morning constitutional. That's Arden, panting and
hurtling his way up the stairs. I love him fiercely, especially just
now, the way he likes to lie in bed between us and gaze into my
face while I'm reading, the bedside lamp lighting up the amber
depths of his cataracted eye, which looks like it's covered by a
skim of coconut oil, something white and reflective when the light
catches it. And the fierce thump of his tail on the black maple
floors when we come home and find him awake and waiting for us;
he can't easily leap to his feet to greet us anymore, but he can
pound that tail on the floor with a glorious, regular ferocity.

Walking is too active a word for what we're actually doing, out
on the sidewalk in front of our building—I am standing there and
Arden is wobbling a bit on his shaky legs, looking around, considering what next—when a woman, a stranger, approaches us. She's
moved, it seems, by seeing such an obviously elderly creature, and
asks how he's doing. I say not so great, explain his various ill-
nesses and his concomitant courage. *Courage* may be an imprecise
term; what I mean is that he retains a certain unmistakable pleasure
in living, an interest in things, despite the increasing failures of his

body, of which he is clearly quite aware. Surely, that is a species of courage.

The woman, who's been bending over to pet him, stands up and seems to, at least figuratively, dust off her hands. She says something like, "He's had a good life. Isn't that just lovely, that we're all part of the cycle, we're here and then we go!"

Well, in truth, she didn't say those words exactly, but whatever she said struck my ear with that effect; she wanted to assert that in the great current of being, the particular elderly struggling creature in front of her didn't really matter, that his particular condition was not tragic, because he was just a flash in the great motion of the whole.

To which I wanted to say, though I did not, *Fuck you.*

All right, the woman on the street is (forgive me) a straw dog. I know her statement probably arises out of an effort to control a grief so deep it needs the fencing boundaries of a readily available rationalization for loss. She probably says such things to strangers so she won't start weeping.

But I hate the erasure of individual value in her claim nonetheless, her easy embrace of detachment. Grief, her position suggests, is a failing. It means you won't accept the cycle of life, that you wish always to preserve what *you* love. Why can't you say, well, Arden and Beau had good lives? They were lucky dogs. To love what lives a shorter span than you do necessitates loss, so get used to it.

I am not, resolutely, used to it. Just now death remains an interruption, leaves me furious, sorrowing, refusing to yield. Too easy an acceptance seems, frankly, sentimental, an erasure of the particular irreplaceable stuff of individuality with a vague, generalized truth. That's how sentimentality works, replacing particularity with a warm fog of acceptable feeling, the difficult exact stuff of individual character with the vagueness of convention. Sentimental assertions are always a form of detachment; they confront the acute, terrible awareness of individual pain, the sharp particularity of loss or the fierce individuality of passion with the dulling, "universal" certainty of platitude.

In the last days of Beau's life, when we used to walk to Washington Square in the afternoon, the low, angling sun would enter between buildings and cast a diagonal of nearly rosy gold across half the houses fronting the square, even across the upper half of the trees.

I loved that light, and in some way, it was *his* gold—that same warm suspension, held there in the cold air a little while. And then the whole world would seem divided just that way, half a haze of golden light, and half an inky, magnetic darkness.

Of course, the square wasn't pitch dark where the light didn't fall, simply a more somber gray and rose. Pitch dark, after all, is a beautiful color, like Arden's rich, black luster. But in me, where I kept and carried that pattern of light, it was different: the world seemed split into radiance and a pure, hungry darkness. Because there was that presence—golden, eager, loving, alert—and there was the emptiness that it countered, and I knew so clearly that the gold was failing. Not that gold would go out of the world—of course, that light would still be there, as it has been since the day those houses were built and first interrupted the pour of the winter afternoon sun. And there would be in the world the brilliance of other dogs, many of them, and in them, I'd see Beau's particular gestures and character echoed, I knew that. But nonetheless *my* gold was disappearing, failing before my eyes, and I had no power to intervene; anything I could do to help seemed only to slow it down a little, if even that.

He was a vessel. Himself, yes, plain, ordinary, and perfect in that sloppy dog way—but he carried something else for me, too, which was my will to live. I had given it to him to carry for me, like some king in a fairy tale, whose power depends upon a lustrous, mysterious beast, and who, without that animal presence, will wither away into shadow. I didn't understand till much later how I'd given that power to both of them, my two speechless friends; they were the secret heroes of my own vitality.

We'd turn southward when our walk was done, heading home in the cold, usually just at the deepening hour of twilight, come early in winter, when the world went blue. Before us would loom two tall rectangles of little winking lamps, wavering in the exhaust and turbulence of the air. By day, they'd been merely harsh geometry, dully regular office towers, the city's pillars. But when evening fell, they'd suddenly seem welcoming, a little darker blue than the sky, glowing with evidence of warmth and habitation.

On Sentimentality

*T*he oversweetened surface of the sentimental exists in order to protect its maker, as well as the audience, from anger.

At the beautiful image refusing to hold, at the tenderness we bring to the objects of the world—our eagerness to love, make home, build connection, trust the other—how all of that's so readily swept away. Sentimental images of children and of animals, sappy representations of love—they are fueled, in truth, by their opposites, by a terrible human rage that nothing stays. The greeting card verse, the airbrushed rainbow, the sweet puppy face on the fleecy pink sweatshirt—these images do not honor the world as it is, in its complexity and individuality, but distort things in apparent service of a warm embrace. They feel empty because they will not acknowledge the inherent anger that things are not as shown; the world, in their terms, is not a universe of individuals but a series of interchangeable instances of charm. It is necessary to assert the insignificance of individuality to make mortality bearable.

In this way, the sentimental represents a rage against individuality, the singular, the irreplaceable. (Why don't you just get another dog?)

The anger that lies beneath the sentimental accounts for its weird *hollowness. But it is, I suppose, easier to feel than what lies beneath rage: the terror of emptiness, of waste, of the absence of meaning or value; the empty space of our own death, neither comprehensible nor representable. Not a grinning death's head but something worse: the lifeless blank, a ʒero no one steps around, though we try; repress it and it returns, more hungry, more negating, with more suck and pull.*

Despair, I think, is the fruit of a refusal to accept our mortal situation. Perhaps it's less passive than it may seem; is despair a deep assertion of will? The stubborn self saying, I will not have it, I do not accept it.

Fine, *says the world,* don't accept it.

The collective continues; the whole goes on, while each part slips away. To attach, to attach passionately to the individual, which is always doomed to vanish—does that make one wise, or make one a fool?

Chapter Two

My Beau lived for twenty-four days, his last, in New York City. Of all his life, those days seem most vivid to me, most peculiarly present in memory. Why should this be, out of seven years of pleasures? The way he'd swim out into the tide toward a flung tennis ball, head held above the water, till he'd reach his goal and then strike forward with his jaws in a single, dedicated motion—and later, when we were both worn out, sit on the sand beside me, leaning his damp weight into me in affection and solidarity (a habit that once led to the worst case of poison ivy I've ever had, since he'd come crashing through the rugosa roses twined in shiny, pointy-leafed vines to rest against me). The wild intensity of his race up the steep cliff of a high bluff on the ocean side of the Cape in Truro. The salt-marsh smell rising from his body after a walk in June (there is nothing else in the world that smells exactly like a golden retriever dipped in a salt marsh). A windy winter day in one of those same salt marshes when we hiked out on the path to scatter Wally's ashes, and Wally's mother threw into the water a single long-stemmed rose, and Beau kept deciding to fetch it back—over and over again, shivering, the pale skin under his strawberry blond growing blue in the cold. A sunny February day when my friend Michael and I went walking in the dunes, and Beau, who'd gone off exploring, came thundering down a snowy sand-slope to greet me, his gaze fixed on my face, and I felt exactly like the old woman in Truman Capote's "A Christmas Memory" who exclaims, "Oh, Buddy, I could leave the world with today in my eyes!"

I carry this intricately detailed history, but just now, it has been covered over by twenty-four days. Now it seems we were always walking down the long corridor of the apartment building, onto the slightly grungy elevator, its floor scuffed by the grit of winter boots and shoes, out the lobby toward the open courtyard, where the doorman, a particularly egregious example of the way that a person with very little power will sometimes wield what authority he does have with remarkable diligence, glares at us because he thinks Beau's going to pee on a trimmed hedge that's either his pride or burden. Then into the crowded pedestrian passageway that leads north toward Washington Square, our landscape: late winter afternoon's thin sun, the paths angling toward the circle at the heart of the park, then the dog run with its rich, acrid air, its leaping and bounding and intent watching from the sidelines. I am not sure that Arden and Beau actually *like* the dog run; it is, clearly, a source of deep interest, but they seem to spend a lot of time on the sidelines, eyeing the leaping and playing, the elegant breeds with their extravagant grooming tossed in with the pit bulls and the flop-eared mutts. I think neither of my dogs is up for the fray. I try to imagine what it would be like to go to a public place fraught with the immediate possibility of either sex or fighting. Would that be a pleasure, exactly, would it make you feel more alive?

But today it's only Beau and I, going not toward the dog run but

north to Ninth Street, walking to the vet. Dr. Cain works in the
East Village, blocks away, and our walk takes us through what's
becoming a familiar passage. We refuse the allure of open space
pulling us toward the park, walk on, up University Place—little
anonymous shops, dry cleaners and dress shops and opticians—
then go past the big apartment buildings on East Ninth, across
Lafayette, where the character of the neighborhood starts changing, and then across Third Avenue into the East Village itself:
red tenement buildings, little patches of ice on the sidewalk,
unreadable spray-painted scrawls, razor wire spiraling over a door-
frame, a gray gown in a designer's window, like an architectural
column made of satin. Carvings from Bali, an extravagant shadow-
box display starring plumed hats, like lost bits of costume from
The Count of Monte Cristo. Past the natural pet food store, with its
abandoned cats up for adoption sleeping in the windows, past the
Ukrainian restaurant with its expressionist murals, then the toy
shop.

I love the windows of the toy shop, where a cardboard puppet
theater painted with stars has been set up, Punch and Judy leering
from behind its little velvet curtain. AURORA BOREALIS THEATER,
the glittery cursive over the stage proclaims. Beau stops here, too,
head up, alert, eying the windows—what does he see? Stuffed animals, puppets, a mobile? As if he wants to go in to see the won-
ders. (Sudden odd sensation, a bit of imagining what it's like to be
a father, witness to a child's delight. Reacquainted, thus, with
delight's beginnings?)

Then a Taoist temple below street-level, clutter of antiques, a
fancy boutique where a glamorous small dog in an angora sweater
guards a window with a big vase of calla lilies. Down the metal

stairs, under a walkway to St. Marks Animal Hospital, with its warm, crowded waiting room. A boy with a turtle in a pasteboard box. Two tailored women with a small, carefully brushed terrier; a Latin transvestite with a long-haired white cat in a carrier on her lap, sitting beside her boyfriend, both with an air of impenetrable sadness. An earnest, bookish young man in his early twenties, holding on his lap a shoebox with air holes punched into the sides and top, through which he gazes down at some undeterminable living thing.

The place is crazy busy; the phone rings all the time; the receptionist must interrupt her conversation with everyone who's arriving or departing to answer and make new appointments. Beau is thoroughly interested, and simultaneously on cautious good behavior; he lies down at my feet, head upright, turning from one loved creature to another, taking it all in.

Our turn, finally. Dr. Cain is short, authoritative, speaks quickly, and has the businesslike air of a Harvard MBA; he's probably thirty, a new-school, high-tech vet, white lab coat, but it doesn't take long to sense, beneath his clipped and rapid discourse, the lineaments of compassion. He examines the charts I've brought, info from Beau's old doctor; he describes the blood work that's needed to monitor Beau's kidney condition; he seems to notice that I have been paying attention to what my old vet's been saying and am now conversant in kidney-function levels, low-protein diets. Beau's lost a few pounds since he was last weighed: bad sign. Pinching his coat shows he's a little dehydrated. He holds still for the blood drawing, accomplished by the doctor's holding one front paw in the air while I hold his head; he's hugely cooperative, as ever, but he winces at the first stab, which doesn't, in fact, find the vein; Dr. Cain must do it again, and this time, both he and Beau flinch; the darkish blood starts flowing into the tube, filling the syringe.

It's days before the phone call comes with the news, and it isn't good. Kidney counts elevated, too much creatinine in the blood. What there is to do: keep the protein in the diet very low, and he should begin receiving fluids beneath his skin. Beneath his skin? The doctor means that a saline solution should be introduced directly into his bloodstream. He says dogs on fluids "stay around a lot longer." I can bring him to the vet's office for this procedure every day, or I can learn to do it myself. "It's easy," he says, "if you can handle it." Dr. Cain says he'll have the technician teach me.

We make the walk again. New faces in the waiting room, new dogs curled on the floor or held on laps, new cats peering out from their carrying crates. The technician calls us in. She's in her twenties, kind, and she looks at Beau with a look I've not seen directed toward him: the sort of pitying look we give to the dying. I remember, all at once, when I met this look before—when Wally first took a trip into town in his wheelchair, after he'd lost the use of his legs to a viral brain infection, a complication of AIDS. That afternoon I knew that other people saw him as dying. There is no reason in the world this should have been a surprise, but still it was stunning, seeing my own reality so directly stated in the eyes of others. It's the look—wordless, freighted with meaning—that makes our experience feel real. We know ourselves by how we're known, our measure taken by the gaze of the outsider looking in.

Today my instinctive response is not to acknowledge this, not quite. On we go, to do what needs to be done. "Fluids"—saline solution, electrolytes—come in plastic bags marked with measuring lines, like the indicators on a measuring cup. The bags must be hung high in the air, so that the liquid can drip through a tube, propelled by the force of gravity, and flow through a needle inserted beneath a dog's skin. The idea is to grab a clump of that nice loose skin that dogs carry on their backs and insert the needle just so, so that it doesn't enter the muscle or come out the other side. It takes practice—both to get it right and to deal with one's own aversion to poking a thick needle into a living body.

Beau was nervous and didn't want to lie down, so we tried it standing up. First I'm too tentative with the needle, and don't poke hard enough. Then I poke too deeply, pinching up a mound of skin so that the tip of the needle comes out the other side. He flinches slightly but doesn't seem to mind too much. I think I'll never get this right, but I try again. The needle's in, but the life-giving waters aren't flowing; the technician says to move the needle a little, as it must be pressing up against muscle, and I do—then, blessedly, the liquid starts to flow. Or rather, to drip slowly; it takes five minutes or so for a bag to drain. We wait. Beau's patient, in his accommodating way, though I can tell by the set of his hips and the way he's holding his head up that he'd like to leave.

"How long," I ask, making conversation, "do we have to do this?"

She says, "For the rest of his life."

I haven't really considered this. This is going to be part of each day from now on? Can I actually do this at home without somebody who knows what they're doing watching?

Then she says, "Well, we've gotten half a liter in him, that's good for the first time, we can stop now." I pull the needle out from the lump that's formed on his back, where the water's not absorbed yet. A little spurt starts leaking out, tinged rosy with his blood. She hurries to tell me that's normal, not to worry. Suddenly I become aware of how much he's shedding; I am kneeling with my arms around him, and my black jeans and shirt are absolutely thick with his blond hairs. I look down to the floor and see I'm kneeling in the bloody water that's leaked from him. I'm on my knees in the ruin of him, and I feel like I can see the parameters of his life in front of me.

I'm kneeling in a bloody room at the bottom of the world and I can see right where we're going, but I push that feeling down, and thank the technician. I buy two big plastic sacks heavy with bags of fluid and needles, and we start to make our walk home. I have one sack in each hand, as well as the leash, and Beau's leading the way, happy to be out of there. But I feel like I'm still in that room, on that floor; I can hardly see what's ahead of us. Though Beau can. He leads us across Fourth and Lafayette, across Broadway; when we're nearly home, someone looks at him with that kind of compassion again—it must be his thinness, the protuberant hip bones, the white muzzle—and something about seeing him reflected in a stranger's eyes entirely devastates me. The resolve I'd had to hold myself together in the doctor's office melts; I'm liquid, my eyes filling with tears so I can barely see the sidewalk.

It's just then that Beau stops and turns his head to look at me, and with a kind of delicate deliberation brings his mouth near my hand, parting his lips just slightly—and snatches the wool glove from my hand. It's his favorite joke, and he goes striding forward with the limp, black thing in his jaws, his tail high and plumed in the air, all happiness. He knows what to do.

Aurora Borealis Theater. The shop window's the only source of light; East Ninth Street's empty and dim. This is the hour when no one's looking, when anything can happen. And so, a show begins: lamps swell behind the midnight curtain; a faint, tinkling music, barely audible through the glass, grows a little firmer and more insistent; then the curtain opens, pulled upward at either side, slowly ascending into the wings. Where are we?

The chamber of a scholar, an aging man who comes here daily, into his sanctum sanctorum of books, a privacy in which he's surrounded himself with evidence of passion: dictionaries, shells, bird bones, feathers, nests, jars of shards, bits of the places he's been, physical testimony. He's reading at his desk, his puppet hands turning the pages of a large, old book, and then slowly his gaze seems to change, slowly his head begins to lower toward the desktop, like an object moving through water or oil, toward the book. His hands come together in front of him on the open pages, his forehead comes to rest upon his hands. Stillness, silence.

Then we watch—it isn't so much terrible as wonderful, how the top of his head springs open, as if the skull had two doors that could fly open like loading docks in a city sidewalk. Inside there it's dark, and then that darkness gradually fills the stage, until the whole space before us is the inside of the scholar's dream.

One thing after another begins to float by, random, the odd apparitions that float unbidden through his thoughts. Shoes, keys, an old kite. Lost articles: a child's beloved pocketknife, owned very briefly, with a horse's head embedded under a bit of domed glass in its handle, handsome profile ringed by lucky horseshoes and green clover. My grandmother's rose-gold wedding ring, my mother's turquoise bracelet, a denim jacket I embroidered when I was sixteen. A pair of handmade leather moccasins, their buckles cinched by round brass rings, stolen at the Yippee Free Festival in a downtown park in Tucson, Arizona, in 1969. Where are these things going, hurrying by in the silent whirlwind? Down the tunnel of disappearance—no, not down, but *up*: here things are sucked up and out of the world, one after the other. Here come some of the objects from his study: that bird's nest collected one winter, in a thicket on the Cape, with a single empty blue egg inside. A love letter received and never acted upon. Sheet of marbled paper from Venice. A box of books and papers lost on one of our moves, containing my passport. It's a sort of cozy whirlwind, strangely, nothing in any great hurry, everything moving past, allowing itself to be seen on the wing.

The scholar—of course, I am that man, with his books and stacks of old manuscripts and archives and clutter—is seeking a position in relation to the tornado. A practiced accounting of each flying element? A discipline of detachment? A study of the human work of cataloging and accommodating each absence? Each body moves upward and outward, in the oldest story. Nothing stays. But something's in my hand, I'm holding on, what is it?

I'm back on the street, looking through the window, staring at the cardboard theater's closed curtain. The weight in my hand's a leash, of course; I look down at my feet, and there is my golden companion, sitting up alertly, gazing at the space where the play has been with complete attention.

On Being a Fool

*T*he wind that blows lost things away, in my dream of a puppet
play, blows through this poem of Emily Dickinson's.

The Wind did'nt come from the Orchard—today—
Further than that—
Nor stop to play with the Hay
Nor threaten a Hat—
He's a transitive fellow—very—
Rely on that

If He leave a Burr at the door
We know he has climbed a Fir—
But the Fir is Where—Declare—
Were you ever there?

If he brings Odors of Clovers—
And that is His business—not Ours—
Then He has been with the Mowers—
Whetting away the Hours
To sweet pauses of Hay—
His way—of a June Day—

If He fling Sand, and Pebble—
Little Boy's Hats—and stubble—
With an occasional steeple—
And a hoarse "Get out of the Way, I say,"
Who'd be the fool to stay?
Would you—Say—
Would you be the fool to stay?

The poem begins in a playful, almost childlike mood—this is a wind that doesn't stop to "play with the hay" or to "threaten a hat." But Dickinson swiftly takes her poem deeper—as is often the case, she works with a light surface in order to startle us with the extraordinary ferocity and gravity at which the poem arrives.

This wind isn't an ordinary one; it doesn't come just from the nearby orchard, but from some more distant, less knowable locale. It's the wind of contingency, and it might bring evidence of distant possibilities, though what it carries to us can't be fully known (that Fir is Where?) or controlled. What the wind brings us is his business, not ours; it isn't within the scope of human power whether he flings at us fragrance or sand, pebbles or steeples or skyscrapers. The wind blows where it pleases, acts as it chooses; anything can, and will, be blown away, and therefore it's a fool's errand to hold on. Who would be that sort of fool, who won't let go of attachment because all we're attached to will be stripped from us?

The implication of the last three lines—with their repeated lingering over the question—is not only that the speaker in this poem is herself that sort of fool, but that she knows her reader is, too. There's nowhere to stand, outside of that wind. But how can one live, being battered and blown again and again? How does one keep agreeing to fall in love over the long haul of erasure?

Chapter Three

This morning, in front of the post office on Eighteenth Street, a reddish golden retriever sat with her leash looped around the iron scallops of a tree well. She was completely focused on the absence of the person who'd gone in to mail a letter; I suppose it isn't even right to call this an "absence," since for her the owner is so palpable a mental fact that she can really admit nothing else: the beeping mail truck backing up, the jackhammering and tar-rolling in front of the new condos across the street, not even the immaculate small terrier clipping by, his legs practically blurring with their unlikely speed. Not a glance. I've knelt down a few feet away to study her concentration. Her forehead is wrinkled a little, a bit of worry or concern—then she turns to me, makes eye contact, a sudden disarming, winning smile, which may just as well mean *Who are you?* as *Hello!*—and then she immediately turns her head back to the task of watching the bronze door of the post office as if her life depended on it.

Which it does, actually.

I mean this physically, in the sense of shelter and food, and of the dog's position in an incomprehensible environment—just what would an unsupervised retriever do on Eighteenth Street in Manhattan?—but I mean more than that, too. The dog exists in relation; her identity has been built around a particular person or persons, a set of social circumstances. They are, to put it grandly, her ontological ground, the location of who she is, from which all possibilities of action and all choices arise.

This accounts for the terrible depression of dogs in shelters, and their evident eagerness to make contact, those who still have the will to do so. I once wrote a poem about the animal shelter in Brewster, Massachusetts, which is where I found Beau. I tried to describe these abandoned ones, and to do so with the kind of double meaning that poetry allows through the breaking of the line, which invites us to hold multiple meanings in mind. I wrote:

No one's dog is nothing
     but eagerness ...

I mean that both ways. *No one's dog is nothing,* in the sense that there is no relationship in which these dogs can ground themselves, to build a set of relations which are, one might argue, dogness. And I also mean the statement to be read all the way through: *No one's dog is nothing but eagerness.* Readiness to begin again, to connect, to start over. It's amazing how even beaten dogs, creatures subjected to the most mindless cruelty, will often seem to say to us, *Yes, I register you, hello, what are our possibilities?* Unless this characteristic freshness and responsiveness are wounded out of them, and they collapse into despair.

Why do we love a species so dependent upon us? It isn't unusual for human beings to actually shrink from expressions of dependence, especially in other people: we dislike a display of need, the acknowledgment of powerlessness.

We are not helping our dogs move toward independence, as we do with children—and as, of course, children long to do. The dog's need for us is permanent. The great evolutionary success of their species lies in their ability to convince us of our need for them.

They have accomplished this by making themselves extraordinarily appealing. It is no easy matter to get at the source of this appeal, which exists at levels beneath the verbal, deep within ourselves. But I can point to some aspects of our delight—seven of them, to be exact.

One

The eyes. The gaze that registers us, fascinated, devoted, characterized by an absolute, unqualified interest. The dog's look registers whatever strikes it, whatever matters. In the country, this seems to be practically everything, every bit of noise or motion. The urban dog learns to select, from the great city wall of stimuli, the interesting ones. But the *most* interesting other for the dog—or at least so we fervently hope!—is ourselves.

A woman on my block walks a squarish, solid retriever named Hartley every day. Hartley is strikingly handsome and magnetic; he draws the interest of passersby, but the woman likes to simply keep walking. Once or twice, I have expressed delight in Hartley, greeting him, kneeling down to acknowledge his broad chest and handsome, chunky paws, the finely white teeth and splendidly pink tongue that he flicks toward my beard. I think this expression of attraction would have been acceptable to the woman Paul and I have called, because we don't know her, "Hartley's mother," had

Hartley not so clearly returned my attraction. He sat in a strikingly upright pose and looked into my face; he offered his paw; he rose on all fours and leaned toward me, putting his weight right against my body, a favorite retriever gesture of affection. *I will let you feel the pressure of me, the physicality of my regard for you—* something like that seemed to be communicated, and Hartley's mother was not pleased. Whether she said or merely indicated, "That's enough, Hartley, time for our walk," I don't remember, but it was interesting to feel that both I and the dog had been chastised—I for intruding, presumably, upon the love of her life. And Hartley? For sharing his open gaze, which ought to be directed solely toward his mistress? Perhaps she depends on Hartley's steady regard to fix her—in many senses of that word. To *fix* her position in space and time, since being known locates us, and to underline her identity as one who cares for, as one who is central, as the subject at the center of her world. "I am I," wrote Gertrude Stein, "because my little dog knows me." But if her little dog should one day turn his look to someone else? Hartley is, after all, *her* mirror, and one's own reflection is necessarily a somewhat private affair.

Two

Much has been said of the dog's nearly absolute refusal of judgment. You never have to dress up for them, they have no sense of human social status, they care nothing about race, economic level, gender, sexual orientation, or any human form of privilege. How useful Arden and Beau were to me after Wally died—not only because their daily needs kept me tethered to the ordinary world of responsibility and schedules, but because I could talk and cry to them for half the day and they didn't mind in the least, never found me morbid or fixated, and never once indicated that I should get over it.

When we talk about this unconditional acceptance, we are really describing a fixity of devotion, a deep reliability. The source of this is, in part, the dog's lack of agency; they cannot really do otherwise than to love us, can they? But that's a negative way to express the fact that by entering into relationship with them, we become that ontological ground I described earlier. The contract that we enter into is one that dogs take with ultimate seriousness. We may choose—we often, sadly, do—to abandon them, to relinquish our side of the bargain, but dogs do not regard this as a choice; they intend, one might say, to honor this pact with all their hearts, or perhaps the less anthrocentric way to phrase that would be to say that in part a dog simply is an intention to be with you, to be conjoined. Thus they are the pattern of fidelity—Fido!—the very template of enduring loyalty, of love without the prospect of abandonment.

This characteristic—and its difference from the vagaries of all human love—lies behind the most sentimental representations of relationships between people and animals. I love these stories: the heroic dog in Provincetown who went daily and lay beside his master's grave until his own death came, and now is represented by a beautiful granite sculpture that still waits and watches. He is best visited on a snowy evening, when the white field around him and the dusting on his tail and paws seem to bring the eager, calm face into focus. The nineteenth-century Saint Bernard in a little town in the northwest corner of Iowa, who saved a toddler from the railroad tracks, picking the child up by her nightgown and carrying her out of the way of the oncoming train, and who is remembered, to this day, by his own life-size bronze image beside the old, disused tracks. In both these stories, the fixity of the dog's look was so noted that it seemed to call for preservation, for a replica, so that the eyes of stone or metal may continue in some permanent version of their chosen work.

If I persist in my assertion that sentimentality is a mask for anger, it isn't hard to point toward the particular source behind this brand of sentimentality: that another human being will never bring to us the same unqualified, unconditional regard that a dog does. Our full immersion in language brings with it qualification and condition; once we enter the world of signs, we can never again be so single-minded.

The fact that I know that stories of faithful dogs are kitsch does not in the least diminish their power. When Wally was ill, for instance, stuck in a rented hospital bed in our living room, losing his mental faculties to a progressive viral brain infection, he liked to watch kids' movies, so I'd rent videos for him, which he could play again and again. As soon as one was finished, he had absolutely no memory of having seen it, and was perfectly happy to watch it again. I bought some headphones for him, so his movies wouldn't drive me crazy. When he watched the Disney remake of *The Incredible Journey*, a tale in which two intrepid dogs and a cat make their way back to their human family through one tight squeeze after another until the inevitable reunion, I made sure he wore them. I didn't want my mind to be infiltrated by those images and their soundtrack, because I knew they'd break my heart. Never mind that my circumstances were already genuinely heartbreaking; I was managing that, somehow, but what I couldn't bear was the *representation* of the heartbreaking.

A little while later, I happened to be on an airplane, on my way home from some business trip, and what should be playing on the screen but *The Incredible Journey*. I managed not to look at it *all* the time at least, though in the final moments, I was riveted. When the old golden retriever finally greets the red-haired boy, his special friend, whom he's been journeying to find again, just the picture was enough to send the tears streaming down my face. I tried to use my Kleenex discreetly, so my seatmate wouldn't see me quietly coming unglued.

When I finally did hear the ridiculous soundtrack, in which human actors voiced the thoughts of the dogs, I thought, well, thank goodness, this is too dumb, too heavily anthropomorphized to be moving, so I'm safe. And then that last scene rolled around, and the old golden, putting his paws on the beloved boy's shoulders, said in his dopey voice, *I thought of you every day,* and that was all it took to turn me into a helpless puddle of weeping, even if I was laughing at myself a moment later.

Three

The soundtrack of that movie is ridiculous because the dogs are speaking, and, in truth, the silence of the species is one of the secrets of their appeal. Of course, they make sounds—a range of them, whimper to growl to full-throttle bark—but anyone who loves a dog has had the experience of being looked at by a creature who seems to be on the verge of speech, or who seems to wish to speak.

Arden has a vocabulary of at least a dozen words, which seems remarkable for a creature that not only doesn't speak English but does not employ language at all, or at least isn't supposed to. Nonetheless he is quite clear on the meaning of *walk, leash, beach, store, sit, biscuit,* and the names of our two cats, Portia and Thisbe.

(Cats, you ask? What cats? Well, no story can contain every-thing.) Asked to find Wally, he would go and do so; told to look for Mark, he makes no mistake about who's who. The phrase "Go pee once" he understands to mean "Go outside, relieve yourself, and come right back in, okay?"

I used to keep a string of brass bells hanging on a rope on the kitchen door. When he wanted to go outside, Arden would go and ring the bells, knocking them with his muzzle. He understood, thus, bell-ringing as a sign. That is a form of language, obviously, since there is no necessary reason that the ringing sound should mean *that* instead of something else. The assignment of meaning is arbitrary, save for the fact that the bells happen to be on the doorknob. There is something poignant about this pushing into the world of speech, signaling.

But he will never himself pronounce a word. Maybe dogs remind us of that verge, that passage from speechlessness; we have each done it individually, as tiny children; at some moment no individual can recollect, we apprehended a word, we attached a sound to an object. That is when we ceased, truly, to be babies.

The bracingly cynical British writer Richard Hughes asserted our distance from the mind of the baby with startling metaphoric aptness:

> When swimming under water, it is a very sobering thing suddenly to look a large octopus in the face. One never for-gets it: one's respect, yet one's feeling of the hopelessness of any real intellectual sympathy. One is soon reduced to mere physical admiration, like any silly painter, of the cow-like tenderness of the eye, of the beautiful and infinitesimal

mobility of that large and toothless mouth, which accepts as a matter of course that very water against which you, for your life's sake, must be holding your breath. There he reposes in a fold of rock, apparently weightless in the clear green medium but very large, suppler than silk, coiled in repose, or stirring in recognition of your presence. Far above, everything is bounded by the surface of the air, like a bright window of glass. Contact with a small baby can conjure at least an echo of that feeling in those who are not obscured by an uprush of maternity to the brain.

And, of course, this is not merely an individual matter; at some point, our entire species took that step, away from wordless participation in experience, into the enabling exile of symbol-making. When we look at a dog who seems nearly pregnant with unsayable meaning, we look back at someplace distantly but faintly familiar.

Four

Dogs offer us a distant relationship to wildness, in an age when we are daily further removed from any such thing; they are a token of domesticated wilderness, of the animal company we have, in the last one or two hundred years, left behind. We are a little startled when our dogs do something out of the domestic framework—swallow a vole, say, or howl at the moon, or roll in shit—but in some way we treasure that, too, and demonstrate how important such moments are by telling other people about them. My friend Marie says she likes our apartment because it has a fireplace that works, and thus we can see, in the middle of New York City, in our own home, the elemental; everything around us is made, but the fire's an inhuman, essential, unshapeable thing.

Are domestic animals a kind of hearth?

Five

Biologists note that we tend to like whatever creature resembles a human infant: chimpanzees, dolphins, and E.T. all partake of this quality. Big heads and eyes, as well as softened features, seem to promptly melt human resistance. The poet Eleanor Wilner takes brilliant advantage of this when she suggests, in her poem "The Love of What Is Not" that the reason anti-abortion activists are so fierce is that the unborn whom they champion actually resemble the way we conceive of aliens, and therefore represent to us the possibility of deliverance. How many science fiction movies turn on the idea that heavenly, unearthly children will come from the sky and gather us up and take us to a new home just before we ruin this one?

Does *everyone* truly want a baby, or a baby substitute? The idea seems reductive. But the truth within it is that we are charmed by certain kinds of limitation: the dog's dependence, like that of the little child, engages rather than repels. There is a certain pathos in the fact that they cannot speak to us, that they can be so fully present without entirely communicating; do we recognize some mirror of ourselves in the way they're embedded in a world of symbols while being only a partial participant in it? Of course, we can speak, we can understand the speech of others—and yet we know, experientially, that only part of our reality is representable in words. I feel immersed in things I can't name most of the time. Try to say what you love about your partner, or what it is about someone that produces in you an intense state of erotic excitement or longing, or even how it feels, precisely, to have a fever—soon it's obvious that we, too, are only partial citizens of the world of language. Something is always escaping; dogs are a kind of figure, an extreme example of that difficulty, and it makes them all the more cherishable.

Six

Then there is the central matter of their relationship to time. Because dogs do not live as long as we do, they seem to travel a faster curve than human beings, flaring into being, then fading away while we watch. An animal's life is for us a theater, in which we may see the forces of time and mortality played out in a form smaller than our own bodies, and more swiftly. An Aurora Borealis Theater?

I came to think about this problem differently when I met two remarkable women from North Carolina, teachers who are involved in the education of veterinarians. It takes a long time to become a vet, and after four years of biology and chemistry, dissection and lab work, students sometimes have a hard time remembering why they ever wanted to be vets in the first place. So, these two have instituted a wonderful change in the curriculum: in the students' fourth year, they spend a semester reading literature about animals, poems and stories and novels centered around the pleasures and mysteries of the human-animal relation. This stroke of genius says to students: *Now that you understand so much of how animal bodies work, you can approach the far-less-quantifiable world of the ways in which this knowledge matters.*

These women pointed out to me some of the fascinating differences between being a vet and being a doctor. A doctor and a patient are a dyad we think of as privileged and inviolable, like a lawyer and a client, a sinner and a confessor; the relationship is a private one. But in veterinary medicine, there's always a third party, the person who's brought the animal to the vet in the first place, and that three-way relationship is the complex arena in which the vet operates, trying to understand the needs of *both* her patients.

To complicate matters further, people live a long time, and, of course, have many physicians along the way. Doctors don't necessarily expect to see their patients through to the end of life. But it isn't unusual for an animal to have one doctor, and for that doctor to stand with the pet's owner from start to finish. The vet's work is to usher human and animal all the way along the arc, and very often to decide when that arc will end—something that American doctors, at least, are forbidden to do with human beings.

In this way, the vet, first meeting a puppy, stands in a position that is an intensification of all our relations to dogs: we are likely to see the small grow larger, to be there for both the bloom and the withering.

The new and the faltering: fifteen years of Arden's body coexist in my awareness, beginning with the awkward puppy who was too little to climb the stairs of our old house in Vermont on his own and had to be carried up to sleep on the rag rug at the foot of the bed, because he refused from his first night to sleep alone. Wally thought a puppy would make noise and keep us awake, so we'd set him in a box in the kitchen with a blanket and an alarm clock, whose ticking, we'd read, would simulate a mother's heartbeat. But Arden would have none of it; he cried mightily, knocked over the box, and proceeded to disassemble the wooden barrier we'd put at the kitchen door—and then stood at the foot of the stairs and cried till we came. Once he was upstairs, he went right to the rug, curled up, and never made a sound the rest of the night. He'd come exactly to the place he wanted to be.

And at the other end of the arc, there's that body struggling again with the stairs: failing hips, heavy breathing from the gray muzzle, steps tentative when the lightbulb was out on the landing because he couldn't see well through those oily-looking, cataracted eyes.

And in the middle—the sleek young adult, ambling through the blazing beech wood some Provincetown autumn when the leaves seem an extravagant spilling over of riches, his big black paws wet with dew, his lovely thick nostrils working overtime, sleek retriever tail in the air. (His parentage remained forever mysterious, since he was found running around with an unrelated older dog on a backwoods farm near Barre, Vermont, and brought to the animal shelter at two or three months old. A Newfie-lab mix? He had the square head, water-resistant coat, and rescuing habits of a Newfoundland, but he was smaller and faster, and loved, as retrievers do, to snatch a tennis ball, though his preferred game was not fetch but *I-have-it-and-you-don't*, which is a terminally unrewarding sport for the one who hasn't got it.)

All these bodies shift through my sense of who he was; all seem to me almost physically available, as if I could in my memory embrace any of those dog bodies, at any stage of our long cohabitation.

To that which travels in time, memories attach, so with the images of that changing body are concurrent images of houses, cities, journeys, passions, errors, and delight. If I remember how it felt to brush Arden's coat into a lustrous shine—trying to go gently, so he'd be patient with me working the tangles out—then I could remember any one of countless times I brushed his coat, but just now it's a night in the West, on a road trip. I can see the bed we lay on that evening, the teal-and-purple bedspread, Paul's head in the next room, reflected in the bathroom mirror, snow whirling around a Colorado motel room on a wild storm of a night. We've pulled off the highway because the blowing drift became so thick we couldn't see, and now it's sifting slowly under the rattling door of the room, howling in the eaves, but we're safe and sheltered for the night, and I am devoting myself to finding every burr and knot in that thick coat—save for the tail, access to which I am not allowed.

To recall his body is to recall its context, a decade and a half of contexts—and threaded throughout them, the presence of two canine participants and witnesses. Their presence marks and organizes time; they're centers around which memory coheres.

Seven

Being human is most likely a much lonelier endeavor than being a dog. Of course, many dogs spend a great deal of their time in solitude, waiting for someone to come home, for the world to begin again—but they live in a state of connectedness, it seems, that we have lost, if indeed we ever possessed it. Is that why we turn to them, they who are always ready to receive, to join in wholeheartedly, as we so often cannot? To be human is to be a watcher; sometimes even at our moments of great joy or great grief there is a part of us conscious of our being, observing that being. I do not think dogs have such a part; they are all right here, involved in whatever it is, and therefore they are a sort of cure for our great, abiding loneliness. A temporary cure, but a real one.

The Photographed Dog

*D*on't all children seem to glow, in photographs? Pictures of children are more radiant than images of our adult selves, because they are less self-aware, less self-monitoring. Pictures of dogs are like that, too. Dogs don't watch themselves from some imaginary point on the outside; they are not split into subject and object, but the camera can stand outside them and look at them in a way they'll never look at themselves.

A few years ago, I was lucky enough to be let into the great archives under the Getty Museum in Los Angeles. The museum owns far more than the glamorous but rather limited public spaces above would ever admit. Thanks to the vast largesse (or guilt?) of the petrochemical magnate, they have a more or less limitless supply of cash to buy virtually anything, and so they do. In the photography archive, there are sixty-five thousand photographs, and the curator was happy to bring out archival boxes, carefully built to seal out humidity, with thin leaves of acid-free paper between each print, and show me some especially compelling photographs of dogs.

Here was the nineteenth-century French photographer Nadar's image of his grizzled pet directly confronting the lens, as nuanced and uncannily present as the photographer's images of Balzac or Theophile

Gautier. Here a comic hound in some anonymous German photographer's fantastical scene, wearing round horn-rimmed glasses and smoking a pipe; how did they ever get him to sit still so long, allowing the lens its necessary long exposure?

And here's Baron von Gloeden in Taormina, with a shot of a naked Sicilian boy looking darkly classical (and not so covertly smoldering) and playing with a black Lab puppy.

And on, into the twentieth century, Lisette Model and Minor White, Paul Strand and Diane Arbus, image after image of beloved creatures caught by the photographer's look, the unself-conscious being given a kind of externalized awareness through the presence of the recording lens.

And not just unself-conscious, of course, but also existing in a different relation to time. These gone dogs look back at us from the continuous present; they are startling right now, full of immediacy and expectation and presence. The elapsed years between their look and ours have no meaning for them.

It helps, of course, that they don't wear clothes. Old photos of people look quaint or dated because of the wardrobes of their subjects; the dog's as naked as ever, as plain as today before the lens.

Robert Giard, a photographer who specialized in beautiful portraits of writers, once wrote: "Photography is the face of our mortality." This portrayal of the mortal, oddly enough, is accomplished by doing nothing; the photograph just waits, fixed, as time passes around it, and before you know it, the image is the face of someone far older now, and then of someone gone. We move further and further from the look that stares out at us from the printed image.

I have a picture I bought at an antique store for fifty cents, a little snapshot aged to sepia, with a scalloped white border. It's a picture of an Airedale, head cocked alertly to one side, ready to play. I like that someone watched that face, and thought it worthy of recording; someone gave form to that watching in this picture. This dog—I don't know whose, or even when—has not become, as old photographs of people do, meaningless; the little terrier has not become no one, deprived as he is of history and context. That is because he was always just this: eagerness, a will to play, a quick delight in returning the gestures made in his directions, a pure readiness.

Chapter Four

My first dog looked like a Steiff toy: stiff fur like a man's brush cut, brave little legs, glassy brown eyes with deep black pupils. He was a collie-and-shepherd mix, a tiny puppy, maybe six weeks old, caramel and white and black, with a lustrous black nose. My father brought him home to the big old farmhouse we rented outside of Nashville the year I was four or five. We lived in the middle of acres and acres of pasture for our landlord's horses; around the white house with its wraparound porch were old outbuildings, where I wasn't supposed to venture, for fear of copperheads. The nameless horses roamed the field and wandered up to the house, and one of them made my parents mad by scraping the paint on our Chevrolet with its teeth, heaven knows why.

I named my puppy Wally, after the older brother on *Leave It to Beaver*, because I liked either the name or the character's plain white T-shirts and wavy dark hair. Of my dog, I remember only his illness; suddenly he was mewling, spitting up. My parents moved him into the old chicken coop. He lay on a braided rag rug we'd brought out from the house. In the way that early memories revise and stage scenes, this one is very carefully lit: just the oval rug illuminated, on the dirt floor of the gray wooden coop, little slats of light between the boards in the walls, and my puppy curled in the center, my mother kneeling down to feed him from a spoon. She'd beaten a mix of milk and eggs in a bowl. When he died, they said it was because he'd had his shots too soon, he was too young. We lived in the country, and animals died all the time, but apparently I was inconsolable; I remember my parents saying, *Mark shouldn't have a dog.* I must have unsettled them somehow with the intensity of my grief, an experience that was repeated when I wept bitterly, a few years later, after I finished a sad book, and my father instructed me to read no more of them.

The black puppy was too big for the little cage in which he was housed, and when the attendant at the shelter first let him out so we could meet him, he promptly fell over, then scrambled up and hurried back in. The long-haired boy, a student at the local alternative college with astonishing eyelashes as black as the dog's lustrous coat, reached in and lifted him back out. "That's the only security," he said, "that little guy has ever known."

This is the point where love, the very beginning of love, shades right out of language's grasp. Could I ever say what made him immediately endearing? Some constellation of image and gesture, some quality of soul, something charmed and promised. Maybe we should be glad, finally, that the word can't go where the heart can, not completely. It's freeing, to think there's always an aspect of us outside the grasp of speech, the common stuff of language. Love is common, too, absolutely so—and yet our words for it only point to it; they do not describe it. They are indicators of something immense: the word *love* is merely a sign that means something like *This way to the mountain.*

≫≪

Ah, but now I remember I've left something out: there's a dog missing from my chronology. I'm maybe four, and we live in a different big house in Tennessee, one on a hill, with a steep gulch beside it where my father's pickup truck is parked, down by the chopping block—a wide old stump—where on some Saturdays he kills a hen for my grandmother to pluck and roast for Sunday dinner. Still completely clear to me, the pale body of the hen, resting in an oval enameled metal roasting pan, black and flecked with little stars, as if the hen lay in the midnight sky.

My sister's boyfriend, of whom my parents do not approve, gives her a gift, a feisty and handsome boxer whose name is-could it be Bo? (Long ago, and never talked about again.) Bo likes to climb up on the porch swing and sit in our laps when we swing back and forth in the cool evening air and sing hymns. One night he's jumping up and gets his paw caught in the space between the slats on the porch swing, and my mother tries to free him, but he misunderstands her intent and sinks his teeth into her arm: purplish bite like a half-moon.

Is it the next day when we're in the car, our old green Studebaker, driving into the country? My sister and I in the back seat, my parents up front, I can't remember where Bo is, sitting with us, on my fourteen-year-old sister's lap? And then we pull over someplace, on the edge of some grassy field, and my father opens his door and then lifts the dog out, and sets him in the grass by the shoulder of the road. Then we're quietly driving away. The memory's the barest sketch: does anyone speak, do we look back?

The sign my father has written in the atmosphere of our family says, *This way away from the mountain.*

How do you tell a puppy's life? Peeing inside, when we get busy and forget to take him out on time, and the yellow pee running in a quick line down the old house's sloping floor. Receiving lavish praise for peeing outside. Beginning of a sense of routine. First bark. In the middle of the night, unexpectedly, a single, wolfish howl, never to be repeated; we decide it's a sign of a UFO passing over. First friendship with another dog, in this case, a pit bull called Shadow, who lives between our house and the railroad tracks and river. Shadow's a tawny, big-headed girl who dwells outside, pretty much unsupervised. As far as I know, she's never been on a leash in her life. She likes nothing better than to wrestle with Arden endlessly. She tempers her own strength; she lies beside him on the grass, and they flash their teeth at one another, and then they lock their jaws together and make growly noises and wrestle with their heads. She wins, very gently, until she lets loose and lets him pin her head down for a moment, just to keep things interesting.

Every day we wander along the railroad tracks by the river: slender birches chewed by beaver, who sometimes slap a tail on the water, great blue herons perched on a rock in the fog, a big, collapsing red barn full of—what? Strange little handcarts that come and go on the tracks, and every once in a while an actual train, a chain of rust-red freight cars, a wave from the engineer. We make a new friend, Beth, who wears a suede jacket with long fringe in all kinds of weather and walks two fat Labs, Bear and Snowflake, their names signaling their colors. When Beth goes into rehab, we walk her dogs, fetching them from her crowded apartment and walking down to the riverbank. It's February, and there's a two-week spell when it's thirty below zero every night, but Bear and Snowflake are used to going out before bed, so we put on a serious number of layers of clothing and trundle down the dark sidewalk to her place. Then Wally and I and the three dogs march down to the railroad path, the five of us walking in a straight line, under a dome of stars glistening like ice chips overhead, and ice below us, too, the snow packed down to a hard, gleaming surface. It's so cold that when the town clock rings out—eleven o'clock—it seems as if the air itself might crack, or the bones in our cheeks. Beth's left a stock of little cups of Hood vanilla ice cream in the freezer, and that's the thing she most wants us to do while she's away, no matter how cold it gets: make sure the dogs have their late-night treat.

As Arden grows, he and I take to walking to town via the back way, following the railroad path, then padding along the busy-for-Vermont sidewalks to the video store, the bank, the bookstore. One day, Shadow's out in the more or less junkyard she inhabits, and ready to play. She tags along on our walk, loping with Arden or with me, enjoying herself, and when we get to the intersection where our path joins Main Street, right beside the two-lane bridge, I tell her to go home, but she ignores me. I point, gesture, try to sound firm. She sits and looks as if she might consider obeying me.

Arden and I walk toward town, and it isn't till we reach the stationery shop whose windows Wally has decorated with constella-

tions of notepads and pens and office supplies, probably the most
boring display job conceivable, that I turn around and realize
Shadow is at my heels. Why I don't just turn around at this point
and go home I can't recall, but I've spent half an hour walking to
town and there must be something I am bound and determined to
purchase. I loop Arden's leash around a parking meter and duck
into the health food store—I'll only be a minute—but while I'm
standing in line to pay for my fair-trade coffee beans or echinacea
drops or whatever it is, I see a streaming blur race past my feet,
and then that same wild force goes streaking up and down the
aisles, racing between people's legs, probably knocking over a
barrel of unsulphured raisins or unprocessed oats along the way.

Since I'm teaching at the ridiculously time-consuming alternative
college, Wally and Arden spend lots of time together on their
own. He's often home, making display-window props for the
stores he dresses in Burlington and Glenns Falls, trying out ideas.
So, the two are always together, and Arden receives such a steady
light of attention that his already incipient character blooms.

A dog seems to come with a temperament attached, the way children do. The swirling forces of environment impress themselves
upon the fresh page of a new personality, but anyone who's been a
parent or a preschool teacher, or has adopted a puppy knows what I
mean: there is a stamp of thisness, of idiosyncrasy that's plainly evident from the get-go. Arden came with a meditative, observant dis-
position, a way of looking off thoughtfully which communicated a
reflective demeanor, and an absolute desire to please and indicate
that *of course* he knew the right way to behave.

I too dislike the anthropomorphizing of animals; there is something diminishing about a dog in sunglasses, something shameful about a rabbit in a straw hat. Such gestures bleach out otherness; they presume knowledge where no such thing is entirely possible, or at least not easily won.

But we'd be equally reductive if we refused to grant animal consciousness its complexities. Who hasn't observed a dog being sneaky, or turning on the charm, or licking her lips in anxiety, or dissolving into complete happiness? And what vocabulary do we have for the life of feeling but our own? I am willing to grant that the emotions of dogs are not like ours, but I'm absolutely convinced that what they experience *is* emotion—and that some of the terms we'd use to describe a human character (observant, thoughtful, desiring) are the best we can do to name their not quite knowable inner lives. (Tolstoy, the master of omniscience, seems to have agreed: there's a wonderful moment in *Anna Karenina*, when Levin's hunting dog, Laska, grows exasperated as her master wastes time in conversation with another hunter, Prince Oblonsky, while a woodcock appears: "... Laska, her ears pricked up, kept glancing at the sky and then reproachfully at them. 'Found a fine time to talk!' she thought. 'And there's one coming ... There it is all right. They'll miss it ...'")

When Arden was six months old, we took him for a hike back through the woods to a swimming hole on a little river behind the school where I taught. As usual, there wasn't a soul around, and we were blissfully skinny-dipping in the waist-high water and wondering if Arden would ever try swimming. So far, he'd merely stood on the edge of any stream, looking in with an equal degree of curiosity and doubt. I decided to float on my back, the brief

Vermont summer sun delicious, the cool water swirling around my ears, when—crash and flounder, suddenly there's a puppy in the water, and said puppy has his jaw quite gently clenched around my shoulder, and I am being rescued and pulled the four feet to shore! How to understand that act: instinct triumphing over fear, the ancestors' tradition of marine rescue written in the genes? A felt sense of responsibility?

There's something refreshing about such virtues sitting beside what might be taken as their contraries: a stubborn streak of independence, a firm notion of boundary. When Arden gets a nasty pad cut, inflicted by jumping into a bog in the woods at the bottom of which lies—a piece of broken glass, rusty tin can?—we hurry to the vet, since a pad cut bleeds all over the place, and he's promptly examined, with us by his side. But we're not allowed to be in the room while the actual stitching up takes place, and when the vet emerges to tell us Arden's fine, we ask, How did he do?

"Well," she says, "he did snap at me while I was working on the stitches."

It seems so out of character that I'm full of disbelief. "He tried to bite you?"

She pauses a beat. "Well," she says, "he's not above it."

Arden has to wear one of those plastic lampshades around his neck, to keep him from yanking out the stitches with his teeth. Either he knows he looks ridiculous or he loathes the limitation the collar creates. He suffers a deep indignity. He stands with his head turned toward the floor, so that the lampshade rests on the painted pine floorboards, the picture of canine dejection. We relent, we remove the lampshade and move his head away from his back paw when we see it tending in that direction. Then, deciding to trust him, we run out for fifteen minutes, for coffee or a quick turn through the video store, only to return and find him on the couch, the black stitches yanked out, the paw cut bleeding away.

Back to the vet, who this time thoroughly sedates him before she goes anywhere near that paw.

Thus begins a lifelong history of Arden and veterinarians, who never seem allowed to see his charming side; in the doctor's office, he's nervous, exasperated, and self-protective. Vets like to offer him a little treat, some liver-flavored vitamin or diminutive biscuit; Arden accepts them, eyes the vet and me, and then delicately spits them out.

One kennel we visit seems like a jail for pets, with concrete floors and brilliant fluorescent lights and awful metal doors that bang and reverberate through the metal walls. The search for an acceptable kennel isn't an easy thing, but there's a week we have to be away. A friend from school recommends Arlene's, a place perched way back on a dirt road on a hill above the college, in a zone of trailers and odd little "manufactured homes." My colleague says, "It might not be quite what you're used to." We call, then go for a visit. Arlene is a wide woman in a flowered dress, who seems to have a bit of difficulty standing; she says, "My leg's been bugging me, but Junior can take you out to the kennel."

Junior is a thick fellow, arms and legs of the same size, and his head seems made of identical material, as if he were built of tubes of clay all extruded from the same pipe. We walk across the muddy patches and the thin grass out back, to a row of pens made of wire fencing, roofless, each one with a little wooden house inside. One pen has several of the ramshackle structures, for the more social. It looks like the canine version of a town in a John Waters movie, but we try to remind ourselves that what we seek in a kennel might well not be the things that would please a dog, and Junior does seem affectionate with the animals, and the creatures wiggling their butts in the pens are completely fine.

When Arden arrives, he appears to find the place delightful. He runs up to the edge of the cages, greeting the inhabitants: much tail-wagging, sniffing, friendly little barks. We're wretchedly nervous about leaving him—I suddenly feel very gay and very middle-class—but he shows no signs of being the least bit bothered, and we're disciplining ourselves not to look back too much as we walk away, letting him be absorbed in his new social life in the big damp pen.

Of course, we call Arlene from San Francisco, a couple of days into the trip. She's as laconic as an old Vermonter could ever be. She says, "He's just fine."

What I want, naturally, are some details, but I don't quite know how to ask for them. "So he's okay?"

"He's doing just fine."

I try again. "He's adjusting okay?"

Pause. Arlene calls out, "Junior?" Another pause, shuffley noise, phone bumped or dropped, muffled words, then, "How's that new black dog?"

Muffled word. She gets back on the receiver. "Junior says he's just fine."

I have no choice but to believe, though I also can't help but imagine Arlene rolling her eyes.

At last we're back, and make the drive from the airport straight up Arlene's dusty, gravelly road. The noise of our car pulling into the driveway rouses Junior, who emerges and leads us out back; Arden's in the big pen by himself, as all the other dogs seem to have gone home. He comes bounding out of his doghouse, and when Junior opens the door to the pen, he jumps straight up in the air, arcing his body like a leaping fish, the picture of joy. Junior retrieves the blanket we've left with him, which feels very damp, as, indeed, does Arden. I look back and see that the doghouse has a gaping black hole in the roof. Arden's been sleeping in the rain all week!

But, in fact, he seems none the worse for wear, perhaps even refreshed by the experience, as happy and eager as he's ever been, though we don't ever go back to Arlene's.

It's fifteen years later when Paul and I drive Arden, on fall weekends, down to a little house Paul's parents own on the Jersey Shore. When we pull off the Garden State Parkway at the exit, Arden sits up in the back of the station wagon, excited, head to the glass, nostrils pulsing at the salt air.

At the house, he's in heaven; there's a small grassy yard that fronts onto a lagoon, a world of things to watch. Arden's happiness is to lie on the grass, watching, alert to seagulls and egrets, to passing boats, to rippling water. Across the canal, they're building condos smack out into the wetlands, so there's an occasional truck, a bulldozer flattening reeds. He hardly has to walk at all if he doesn't choose to—it's hard for him, these days—and a whole world seems to offer itself for his inspection. Eventually he falls asleep, out in the grass, and in a while wakes up and watches again.

He's so pleased with his situation that he doesn't want to come in that evening, so we let him stay there, sleeping in the twilight.

We don't have the heart to wake him up to bring him indoors, but at three in the morning, we're roused by a crashing lightning and then a wild downpour, like gravel poured onto the roof of the house. Suddenly I'm awake enough to think, *My God, he must be miserable!* I pull on some shorts and run out into the storm—only to find him so deeply, completely asleep he seems he might be sinking into the earth. He's soaked to the bone. I say his name— nothing. I stroke him, no response. Now I'm soaked in the cold rain, too. I put my hand on his ribs to make sure he's breathing, which he is—but he has gone so far into the bliss of sleeping in the grass beside the dark lagoon that I can't wake him at all. And this is a dog who didn't even like to go for a *walk* in the rain!

I don't know that in a few minutes, after I've given up and run back into the house to wrap myself in a towel and shiver and shake off the water as if I were myself a large, soaking dog, he'll stumble back into awareness, wake up enough to hobble to the door so that he can have a towel-drying, too. Just now, as I am bending over the absolutely still black body gleaming in the flashes of lightning, he suddenly seems to me the image of King Lear—the mad old man on the moor, fallen, intensely vulnerable, the very image of all our aging, helpless in the storm. And I'm the worried Fool, trying to rouse the tragic, failing King.

But perhaps I dramatize, as I have been known to do. *(Mark shouldn't have a dog....)* I could also have read his deep, dreamless sleep in the rain as a memory of Arlene's, of lovely nights of youth in a fragrant field, in good company, where the rain must have brought to the sleeping animals new fragrances of its own.

Smell of Rain in the Field

*R*ain on the old wood of the doghouses, rain on the spots where
dozens of visiting dogs have slept or peed, rain picking out the
flowers of the field, each with their definite scent, intensifying the odif-
erous leaves. It makes one dizzy, to imagine that universe of particular
smells, and all those fragrances rising together—how encompassing it
must have been, how dense with information!

*Virginia Woolf considers this problem in her biography of Flush,
the cocker spaniel who traveled with Elizabeth Barrett Browning from
stuffy rooms in London's privileged Wimpole Street to the airy free-
doms of rented villas in Pisa and Florence. She names the realm of
scent as a world of perception nearly closed to us, though open to the
nostrils of a spaniel in nearly unthinkable abundance.*

Where two or three thousand words are insufficient for what we
see, *she writes,* . . . there are no more than two words and perhaps
one-half for what we smell. The human nose is practically non-
existent. The greatest poets in the world have smelt nothing but
roses on the one hand, and dung on the other. The infinite grada-
tions between are unrecorded. Yet it was in the world of smell that
Flush lived. Love was chiefly smell; form and color were smell;
music and architecture, law, politics and science were smell. To

him religion itself was smell. To describe his simplest experience with the daily chop or biscuit is beyond our power. Not even Mr. Swinburne could have said what the smell of Walpole Street meant to Flush on a hot afternoon in June. As for describing the smell of a spaniel mixed with the smell of torches, laurels, incense, banners, wax candles and a garland of rose leaves crushed by a satin heel that has been laid up in camphor, perhaps Shakespeare, had he paused in the middle of writing *Antony and Cleopatra*—

But Shakespeare did not pause.

Chapter Five

Late in the spring, ragged, high-cloud day, I'm standing in the doorway of the gym in Provincetown, looking at a bank of purple tulips. The outside of their petals is almost black, with the kind of sheen to them that feathers have, or plums. Some of the petals already dropped away, and even though the afternoon sun's at the exact angle to illuminate the remaining ones from within, there's a wind coming, and darker clouds on the way. I think, *That's it, they aren't going to survive much longer, this is the moment of their glory, this startling just-now ...*

And then I think, *Oh, for heaven's sake.*

~

Me, dramatize? Just a little. I don't mean that I display an overly emotive surface, not that sort of drama. Rather that I am prone to interpretation, and to reading the moment as cosmic evidence, quickly turning things to metaphor. My friend JoAnn says she looks at her own writing with "shit-colored glasses." I wouldn't say I wear *those*, but I am aware that I tend to look at the world through a glass tinted with the awareness of mortality, like those green bus windows that murk up the view to the extent that sometimes you can't quite tell what time of day it is. I did, after all, grow up with apocalyptic Christians who believed the end was near, and that this phenomenal world was merely a veil soon to be torn away. This is great training for a lyric poet concerned with evanescence.

Of course, it's a gift, to know that things have limits; of course, the shadow is what creates three-dimensionality. But I fix on the darker note, and sometimes I think the only kind of beauty I can see is the kind that's right on the verge of collapse. Is that the only kind of loveliness there is?

And here Mr. Beau snatches the glove of my narrative.

(I can't remember exactly when Paul and I began to call him *Mister* Beau. We never really talked about it—it just seemed something to do with the surprising maturity and dignity he attained, halfway through his life, after having been the goofiest mess of a retriever on record. So much so that, the first time I saw a sightless person being guided along by a seeing-eye golden, I thought, *Good luck*. It was a few years before I saw the capacity for sustained attention, even nobility.)

Ho, he says, *enough*.

He likes stories that move along spiritedly; he likes (forgive me) a wag in the tale. Surely, *his* story moved through passages of darkness. When I adopted him, he was a neglected slip of a thing, but his heart was capable of soaring. I call on his spirit when things get logy, when I feel an internal clock slipping into what Dickinson called an "hour of lead." Attention to the mortal shadowing of all beauty—that's a perspective that comes to me too easily, something I have to resist. And that's why I loved that heavy golden paw tapping at my knee—*notice me, come back*. A kind of sweet slap, with the blunt tips of his nails poking at me. A slap I miss now with all my heart. Though I internalize it; I try to slap myself, to shake off an excess of somber tones; I need his buoyancy, telling this tale.

An AIDS diagnosis for Wally—well, ARC, in those days—led us to think again about living in Vermont, about the choices we'd made.

Arden wouldn't know a thing of what propelled us to Province-town; the events that shape dogs' lives swirl above their heads, while they stand or sit beside our legs, or lie on the floor, looking up at us. He must have sensed our anxiety and exhilaration and then our intense focus: much sorting and selling, much disassembly of the household, and suddenly, come September, we're living—is it possible?—in a rented cottage on a strip of beach at the farthest narrow crook of land sticking out into the Atlantic. Ours, in fact, is one of the last houses at the very tip of Cape Cod; beyond us there are a couple more cottages, an oddly out-of-place motel with a sixties colonial look in the most spectacular of locations, and beyond that, miles of salt marsh and dune where the promontory spirals down to the slimmest, final curl at Long Point Light.

For us, our new home was itself a beacon: a town where our presence as a couple was both welcome and ordinary, a commu-nity where Wally's HIV diagnosis was nothing unusual. We had company in our uncertainty. We wouldn't be alone with this if things went as we feared they might, who knew how or when.

Arden's new world could hardly have been any more of a wonder: salt flats that stretched for miles when the tide was out, and the bay one vast arena of exploration. The pleasure of merely sitting on a low dune beside the little house, beside a beached cata-maran whose rigging whistled in any wind. From there, any person or dog approaching could be sighted long ahead of time, taken stock of, greeted.

A dog who appears daily is Kringle, a surprisingly butch dachshund from the restaurant next door; he strolls over, butts his head against the screen door to summon Arden, and the two head for the beach in front of the Red Inn, where they roll on their backs in the sand, growling happily, their teeth flashing at each other—a contest between extreme unequals in size, which is sustained endlessly, because Arden doesn't want the tussling to end.

And then there are long walks: to town, along the strand behind the waterfront houses, clambering over stone jetties, sniffing out all manner of beached sea life, into the social whirl of town (that part isn't Arden's favorite; he prefers the approach, not the arrival). In the other direction, out toward the great ocean beach, there is no arrival, merely the paths through thickets of beach plum and dense banks of wild roses, beach grass in ceaseless arcing motion along the dunes that front the sea. The sea! It seems absurd to have a single word for it, as it never on any two days in my history of knowing it appeared remotely similar. An immense continuum of colors—at one end, the water actually black or burnished steel; at the other, a transparent gemstone shade Marianne Moore called "the color of muttonfat jade," a vast rippling of pale green jelly.

Into this Eden for dogs insert one afternoon and evening of terror. Wally and Arden are walking across the grassy lawn of the motel, a strip of green separated from the street by a thick hedge. They're nearly home, so Arden's off the leash, ambling in the direction of our front door, when a rabbit bolts toward the hedge.

Our intrepid hunter bolts after him, right through the thick privet and into the road. Before Wally can even see where he'll have to run to find an opening in the green wall, he hears the sickening screech of brakes, the horrible thud of body on metal: the unmistakable hollowness that something yielding, something with lungs makes, when something unyielding strikes it.

Wally is racing, panicked, breathless; the car that struck Arden has stopped, the two men inside beside themselves, but Arden's nowhere in sight. The guys say he's taken off running, in the direction the car was coming from, toward town; can he really be hurt if he's a ceaseless streak of black racing the wrong way down Commercial Street? Wally sprints after, asks everyone on the street if they've seen him, and someone indeed says they saw a black dog running up Franklin Street; thank goodness he at least isn't running into the center of town—he's heading uphill, toward the dunes? But he'd have to cross the busiest streets in town to get there.

We walk and bike and slowly drive the narrow streets, calling ceaselessly, talking to anyone who's out and about, in case they've seen him. We make signs (BLACK LONGHAIRED RETRIEVER, ANSWERS TO ARDEN, MAY BE INJURED) with our phone number and a sentence of narrative about what happened, to catch people's interest; we copy them quickly and post them everywhere: the bulletin board at the A&P, the signpost in front of the seasonal movie theater, the post office. We drive to his favorite spots: beaches, dunes, woods. Nothing. Night's coming on, and all we can hope is that he's just holed up someplace, in shock, betrayed by the world. We keep saying he's probably not hurt, not if he can run, but who knows really how he is? There's a sort of raw desolation in Wally's voice

I've never heard before, sometime that evening, when he turns from the window to me and says, *Where IS he?*

Terrible, willed sleep (is that what Arden is experiencing, too, wherever he is?) and then, just as we're about to set out for more searching in the morning, the phone rings. Some men from Boston, down for the weekend, are in the open space in front of the bank where our end of town begins when a black dog, looking a bit dazed, comes walking down the sidewalk, a little tentatively, but definitely walking west, toward home. They've seen our poster in front of the theater just minutes before, and discussed it, so they walk over and say, "Arden?"

The man on the phone says Arden stopped in his tracks, appeared to shake his head as if clearing his ears, looked directly at the fellow who'd said his name, and wagged his tail. It's the name that seems to restore him to connection, to the human world, the name that brings him home.

Entr'acte

Dogs and Their Names

*D*ogs have no power over their names, but names have power over
dogs.

*When we say "sit" or "fetch," we mean one thing only, but when
we cry "Scout!" or "Ollie!," we send a signal of more ambiguous
intent. This is a complex kind of linguistic operation, when you think
about it: a sign that must be understood as a marker only, a call to
attend to a situation the exact contents of which cannot be indicated
by a single word. When those sensitive ears prick up to "Joey!" or
"Smoke!" what is meant is* look here, attend, come, stop what
you're doing, listen up! *The spoken name doesn't always mean the
same thing, and whenever it's spoken, it must be considered in context to determine what it indicates this time.*

*A dog who doesn't know his name is in a sorry state. Recognition
of the name is the signal of the bond, the term that denotes the contract. The saddest dogs in the shelter are the ones without any
names—no one even cared to properly give them up. They have
simply been abandoned; nameless, they bear no signature of human
attention. That boxer my father released to the world, all those years
ago—he stopped being Bo the moment our car drove away.*

Benny, Bruno, Coco, Colby, Cowboy, Delta, Diva, Hammer, Jake, Joey, Lola, Luke, Mabel, Maggie, Martin, Mickey Two, Molly, Patou, River, Shadow, Sphinx, Taffy, Willow, Zoey.

Do names have power to shape the character or identity of a dog? Certainly, they shift our perceptions. Parents fiercely consider potential names for their babies in utero, and those manuals that offer (and sometimes evaluate) the possibilities. Blake, Madison, Britney? Not this year. Name your daughter, say, Cassandra or Constance, call your son Butch or Carlton, and what are you saying about that child's future? Names create expectation, call up assumptions about character; they have things to say to us about class, allegiances, gender, behavior.

Dogs, of course, are named after they're born, usually weeks after. And so, that act of naming involves not only the owner making a statement about herself (how will I be seen, calling this name aloud at the park?), but an evaluative judgment as well: the name needs to fit, it needs to sit properly on the new being before us, who already is definitely not Clark or Pierre, who might be Willy or Savoy.

But names are predictive as well as descriptive. If you think of a dog as, say, Macha, if you approach her as such, don't you shape her identity in that direction—since dogs are such superb readers of our expectations? The Macha I knew was exactly that, a tough and athletic Doberman who'd race through the parks of Iowa City like a house on fire; she'd leap out of her pickup truck and dive right into leading the pack that met in the park every afternoon. The strongest yellow Lab I ever knew was called Mike, and his owner used to call him on the hills in Salt Lake in an unmistakable Philadelphia accent: "Moike!" That monosyllable with its heavy final consonant sounded insistently ath-

letic. Two old leathermen who ran an antique shop on the Cape kept their Pekinese enthroned on a chair in front of the shop with bows in her hair: Princess. Such names inscribe a character, fix an identity. My friend Cathy called her rough-and-tumble wolfish Texas dog Lovey, a rich kind of contrast to the look of him, a corrective.

Seabiscuit, Pax, Mrs. Simpson, Mowgli, Lucky, Flute.

The edifice of gender we build around dogs through naming is, in truth, too unwieldy and ridiculous to examine. And it drags along with it a fear of same-sex congress that would be comical if it weren't so often a big deal to those who enforce it. If a male dog sniffs another's hind end, this has nothing to do with what human beings mean when they engage in similar behavior. Dogs must simply add whatever prohibitions we impose to the vast category of inscrutable human actions.

Arden's nicknames: Tiny, Fatty Lump, Lumpy, Mister, Ardenoid, Missy, Li'l P, Beyoncé, the Everlasting Beyoncé. Does he answer to any of these? Well, it's all contextual; he likes to be spoken to, and the particular content of the babble breaking over his lovely head mostly doesn't seem to matter.

Sphinx, the dog who lives downstairs from us in the city, is totally deaf, as far as I can tell. I don't think he can see much, either. When we take him out for a walk sometimes, when his owners are away, what he likes to do is move down the street in his favorite direction, and smell the iron railings around the tree wells. He does this slowly, and can persist a very long time. When we say his name, he doesn't hear us. We get down and talk to him and hug him, and I can tell he likes it, panting a bit, pushing his head toward us, feeling perhaps the familiar vibrations that remind him of the sound of his name.

Chapter Six

Our new house, a block from the harbor, on a narrow, curving lane, is new to us but very old indeed. It's housed two hundred years of inhabitants, only a few of whom we'll ever know a thing about: a Portuguese whaler; a family with eleven children, one of whom grew up to be the town nurse; a lesbian singing group called the Dyketones. For Arden, it offers particularly interesting things: the ancient smell of the old hemlock beams we've uncovered, the mouse-and-cedar scent of the attic, those seemingly empty spaces in the air at which a dog sometimes stares abstractedly, as if some window in the room's atmosphere had opened into other rooms, the world of ghosts and accumulated human presence, which lends to the air of an old house a certain weight, a not-unpleasurable sense of long habitation in time.

Just down the block, along the bayfront, town dogs gather in the morning and near twilight, a twice-a-day pack of leaping and racing pets and sleepy or convivial people with leashes around their waists. One cool, foggy morning, Arden greets a woman trundling down the beach in a heavy, hooded sweatshirt. When she bends to greet him in return, he's so interested in her that he grabs hold of her dark blue hood with his teeth and simply pulls her to the sand, thus commencing a wrestling that the not-so-hapless, laughing woman clearly enjoys—thank goodness! This is how Arden befriends Mary Oliver, a poet whose affection for his species is boundless.

And there's a garden, soon fenced, with just enough grass to roll upon after the detested indignity of a bath (necessitated with some frequency, since skunks wait in the darkness beneath decks and lurk in the thick shade of wild rugosas). The garden allows the extended study of birds, who nest in eaves where the downspout crooks and makes an armature for house-building. Simply sitting there, or lying down facing the street, seems a source of delight, and when the sun warms, there is, ever more inviting as it grows, a dense thicket of forsythia, through which a black muzzle, already showing a dusting of white, often looms out of the shadows.

How does a dog experience the decline of a beloved man?

Walks with Wally are shorter, and then they're fewer. One day, he's just too tired to go at all, and Arden and I go out to the spring dunes alone, a shred of fog blurring the new green, little coppery pools the tide's left behind near the rim of the marsh. I spy a man in the distance, walking toward us, lurching down the slope near the road. That familiar green parka—isn't that Wally coming to join us? My heart lifts more intensely than I'm quite prepared for and then sinks immediately when I see that it isn't him. I didn't know, till just that moment, that he wouldn't be coming with us anymore.

More time resting, curling up on the rug by the couch. The couch becomes the place Wally lives much of the time. Arden walks with me a couple of times a day, trips out to the garden, but mostly he's lying down, in the warm house, voices of TV and the radio building their atmosphere of human community. His back grows a little thicker, the curve from broad chest up to hips not the narrowing arc it used to be. In a while, the couch is moved out of the room, replaced by our four-poster from upstairs; Wally just doesn't feel safe on the stairs anymore. The bed occupies the room almost completely, a big, flannel island, and Arden's mostly to be found curled on my side of the big square, keeping Wally company, keeping watch. When Wally can't leave the house anymore, his therapist comes once a week to visit; she says Arden is Wally's guardian, animal counsel, who quietly and thoroughly observes and considers every coming and going. He would be the angel of protection, were there any way to protect anyone from this invisible, unknowable thing.

Which is a viral infection—some quasi-living bug we all carry in our livers crossing the barrier into the brain. First tiredness; then a loss of visual perspective, so that stairways become dauntingly strange; then more tiredness; and then the legs don't seem to work right, and one day don't work at all.

A procession of people into the house, home health aides, visiting nurses, volunteer assistants, social worker, occupational therapist, all of whom the guardian must consider, assess, admit. He tolerates everything except being asked to leave the bed. If the home health aide wants to administer a bath, or the nurse to give a shot or an exam and would prefer not to have canine witness and company, they're met with a growl, a glare, and, when the objection is defeated, an annoyed sigh, a slinking into the next room, but only for a while. Perhaps he's not so much the guardian as he is the already bereaved; he's been so attached to Wally, who has been there beside him all his life. I've loved Arden dearly, but Wally's been the most available, Wally has been his lodestar. And now he's barely there, and sinking further into the warm, motionless dream of the bed.

Whatever occupies Wally's brain may have paralyzed him from the waist down, but it's not harmed his appetite—which is, if anything, heightened, a yearning for fats and salt. The home health aide makes lavish breakfasts, frying up huge amounts of bacon; it isn't discovered for a while that at least half the bacon strips are going straight into the grateful mouth of the attendant retriever, who grows wider with the winter's waning days.

I was walking down the single aisle of cages—dogs coming up to greet me, barking a bit, or holding back, eyeing me to see what I was up to, all manner of sizes and colors, ears and tails—when I came to a pen in the middle of the room, where a very skinny and very calm golden retriever sat sphinxlike on all fours, serenely looking up at me. He eyed me, and began to thump his blond tail on the concrete floor—a gesture I couldn't know I'd come to love, a greeting and declaration that could be prompted simply by looking at him and beaming the psychic equivalent of "Hey you" in his direction. That thump always seemed to me the physical version of a laugh, a little goofy, a bit dumb, entirely delighted.

But who was he? If he was a golden, he was the skinniest one I'd ever seen, a very narrow head, and his chest so thin that the bone at the center stuck out sharply, the prow of a slender blond boat, and his waist was even narrower. The label on the cage read: BEAUCEPHUS, PART SALUKI? MIX, THREE YEARS OLD, TOO MUCH FOR OWNER.

Awful name.

Saluki? An extremely narrow North African breed, something like an elegant, ethereal cross between a greyhound and a delicate yellow rat.

Three? Too much? Well, if he was full grown, he was a gangly fellow, all sharp bony edges, and if this was too much, I couldn't imagine what calm would look like. I knelt down, and he rose and walked to the cage door, bringing his face near to mine, then he unrolled a long tongue, splashed with purple spots as though he'd been eating blackberries. He lay down again and gazed at me with what I can only describe as an absolute openness, as if each new thing that came into his attention were greeted with the same cheerful equanimity, a curious and cheerful regard. He extended a paw in my direction. My body—heart? impulsive head?—said *Yes.*

What on earth was I doing in the animal shelter, thinking of adopting a dog at a time like this? I hadn't planned it this way. We'd heard through a mutual friend about some fellows in the city who were dealing with some of the same crises we were, and could no longer keep their cocker spaniel. That was all Wally needed to hear; was it because he was becoming increasingly childlike that he wanted some small, encompassable creature to sleep next to him and lick his face? (I couldn't say to him that it was clear that Arden was far too depressed for these duties. I don't think I could even see that myself, in the crisis of those days, when I was trying to hold a collapsing house together.) We agreed. I went to pick up little Dino, but on the front stoop, Jimmi and Tony told me they'd changed their minds, and, of course, I was glad for them that they couldn't let their animal go. But I knew how disappointed Wally would be, and on the way home I found myself pulling off the highway to the shelter, and before I knew it, here I was, on my knees on the concrete floor by the pen, in over my head.

He was, of course, much bigger than a cocker spaniel, but he seemed the calmest, dreamiest dog, the perfect candidate for the required sleeping and licking duties.

He gazed at me steadily, still thumping, and then rose again, walked back over, and put the beautiful weight of his head in my hands.

That did it.

On the way out, I'd learn that this admirable tranquillity was the result of sedation; Beau had been neutered, as was the shelter's policy, and he was just waking up. Never mind, I said yes anyway, and was told the next step would be to bring Arden over to meet him; the shelter wanted to be sure they'd get along.

Back home, I'm ablaze with the news: Wally's excited, if a little bit uncertain about the size of the new arrival, who isn't going to be the cuddly small thing he'd anticipated. My friends think I've lost my mind: *You're taking care of a man who can't get out of bed and you're adopting a golden retriever?* They do have a point, but there's a certain dimension of experience at which the addition of any other potential stress simply doesn't matter anymore. Oh, say the already crazed, why not?

Arden, as ever, is happy to go for a ride, and sits in the passenger seat taking in the landscape, turning to me from time to time, while we drive the half hour to Brewster. It occurs to me that I should be a little nervous about taking him to a shelter, given his history—does he remember the smell, the texture of animal anxiety in the air? If he does, he doesn't indicate it. He waits in the car while I go in and, with an attendant, bring Beau outside, to a small, grassy corral where the two can run around together. The attendant, sturdy in her jeans and hooded sweatshirt, watches from just outside the gate; she wants to see that the two dogs get along. Which they do, just fine, racing around on the grass, greeting and tussling, though I can tell that, in fact, Beau's high energy—he's just been let OUT—is a little startling to Arden. And playing with a stranger in a neutral, outdoor space is quite another thing than said stranger actually getting into your car with you, but I tell the attendant all is completely well. Arden waits in the front seat while I sign the papers and pay the twenty-five dollars, and then I bring our new dog to the car, where he leaps inside and begins merrily bouncing about. Arden commences a quiet, throaty growl, far more threatening than any louder demonstration. I drive out of the parking lot very quickly, my family suddenly one member larger.

Wally's just about to eat his lunch when we arrive. Nancy, the home health aide, has made him a bacon, lettuce, and tomato sandwich with mayonnaise, and when we come hurtling into the room, Beau jumps onto the bed in wild greeting, licks Wally's face exuberantly while Wally laughs and laughs, and then the untutored creature simply consumes the lunch off the plate, every last bite.

Some things I learn about Beau immediately: the pads on the bottom of his feet are pink and soft as human skin, and seem hardly to have touched the earth. He has been living in a crate. He lacks, almost entirely, what psychologists call "impulse control."

He doesn't know his name, or any other word. He is no Saluki mix but a starving retriever, and if he's three years old, he certainly hasn't been fed much, as he immediately begins a process of doubling in size. His appetite is prodigious, boundless. Most days, we walk along the town beach. Off-season, especially in the morning or early evening, when no one's about, dogs walk there off-leash, taking delight in waves and wrack line, splashing into the water. Beau is unnervingly interested in the backs of the houses that front the water, sniffing out more to eat. One day, we're walking past the back of Saint Mary's of the Harbor, where an early church supper has just ended, and the leftovers are being tossed down onto the sand for the squawking seagulls. Who would have thought that a retriever would love baked beans? Vast amounts of beans, pounds of them. I know I should intervene, but I'm so startled by his ardor, by the prospect of this neglected youth suddenly having *enough*, a rich, steaming demonstration of enough, that I can't help but just let him go.

Arden is visibly stunned, albeit too gentlemanly not to be accommodating, and I am consoled in knowing I haven't just displaced him or made him feel put out, because he is clearly, beneath a certain level of mature exasperation, *interested* in Beau. Who is this obstreperous thing? Taking up a great deal of space, socially clueless, but even to Arden, it appears, charming. I know, because on his first day in the house, Beau commences a game with Arden, the sort of head-wrestling Arden used to do as a puppy, years ago, with his pit bull pal in the weeds back by the railroad tracks. Arden and Beau lie on the floor, heads close to one another, and their

teeth flash as they lunge and nip and make horrible noises, a pair of
wolverines in heat; they more or less playfully attempt to bite each
other on the neck, each trying to deflect the other's teeth, so that
often the big ivories click against each other—if teeth could spark,
the house would have burned down. Sometimes the matter gets
out of hand, even for them, and there's a yelp and retreat, then in
a minute they're back at it again till neither one of them can hold
their eyes open.

When we have to rent a hospital bed, I push an old single iron
one up against it so we can still sleep together. If some of the
people who came to help us out are quietly horrified that both beds
are full of retrievers—well, so be it. We've made an island, a
small, very full home.

Beau's never really still until he simply keels over, usually in
bed, and curls himself into a ball like a golden hedgehog, tumbling
headlong into sleep. If I'm worn out with him, if I'm entertaining
the notion that maybe I've made a big mistake, all such thoughts
vanish when I look at that face, awake or asleep. I have never
thought of myself as a patient person, but some new reserve seems
to be appearing within me; I can sit with Wally and talk about
nothing, remind him gently when he's watched the same episode
of *The Golden Girls* three times in a row and found it equally funny
every time, tease him about his appetite, laugh with him when he
can't find the words he wants.

And I have a bottomless reserve of tolerance for Beau. If he
wanders out onto Bradford Street, where in the off-season people
drive a ridiculous number of miles per hour, I'm terrified, but it
happens so many times I have to begin to negotiate with the panic
I feel when he runs; this is part of his wildness, I tell myself, part

of who he is, and if he does get hurt, I'll have done everything I can. But, in fact, he seems to have a charmed life, though once or twice cars must slam on the brakes for him and for me right behind, chasing him across the middle of the road. When I catch up with him, I try to firmly communicate that this was a terrible idea, but, in truth, that wagging tail dissolves both fear and anger. When we go out the back door for a walk, or come in from one, whenever he's off his leash, he's fond of leaping the stockade fence—no mean height—to head for the garbage cans behind us at a little rental compound called Julia's Cottages for Two. I look for him until I find him, usually in Julia's trash, gobbling some old chicken bones, and then he looks up at me and starts swishing that plumy tail back and forth like crazy, all happiness. He looks at me with the plainest, pleased gaze, and what's to be upset about?

This is all a bit like a famous old joke. A man goes to a rabbi for help. I'm miserable, he says, my life is unbearable. What's the matter, asks the rabbi? I have a tiny house, an angry wife, six children, almost nothing to eat, my feet hurt, what can I do? The rabbi says, without raising an eyebrow, Get a goat. This sounds crazy to the man, but this rabbi's reputed to be very wise, so he does it anyway. The next week, he comes back to the rabbi. Help me, he says, the goat is a disaster! The goat eats our clothes, takes up all the space in our little house, my wife is furious, it steps on my feet, what can I do? The rabbi says, absolutely calmly, Get rid of the goat. Next week, the man comes back and says, Oh, rabbi, thank you, my life is wonderful now!

The difference is I love the goat.

One day, when he's sacked out next to Wally, his back close to Wally's hips, I see my lover lift his right hand—the hand he can't use to feed himself anymore—and bring it through the air, with intense deliberation, to rest on Beau's golden flanks. I take a picture of that gesture, because that's the way I want to remember him. Maybe the last thing he ever did with that hand, I don't know. The gesture perhaps not so much for Beau himself—the bounding, confused, happy thing—as toward all he represented: possibility, beginning, potential sweetness, vitality. Dear man reaching to the world: how I want to go when I do.

Graveside

*T*he night Wally died—that wind, from Emily Dickinson's poem, blowing through our bed—Arden had been sleeping with him all day, except for a couple of quick, cold walks. He was entirely gone into his sleep, until maybe fifteen minutes before the end of Wally's life— then, suddenly, he jumped, fell off the bed with a loud whunk on the old wooden floorboards, and slunk off into the next room.

In truth, I don't know where he and Beau were for a while, for several hours. Until, in a diminutive hour of the deep winter night, the couple arrived from the funeral home to take Wally's body away. That was the one thing, after all of this, I could not bear to see; I couldn't let him go without me, not that way. So I took the dogs down to the frozen bay, in the pitch darkness. We wandered around awhile by the swelling dark of the harbor-water, under black sky pricked with the fierce script of January stars, and when we came home, his body was gone.

What is it, to a dog, when a person dies?

Beau was still out of focus, and, in fact, hadn't known the laughing, benevolent, aching presence in the bed in the front room long enough to have much connection to him. But Arden? I'm remembering a batch of photos Wally took, at Herring Cove Beach. Wally's wearing his old scarlet winter coat, holding a tennis ball in the air, and

Arden is leaping up to seize it, a liquid black shape twisting in the air. The series is carefully staged so that each part of Arden's leap is captured, almost like a flipbook, though Wally didn't have that rapid-clicking shutter device fashion photographers use, so he must have done this in the most painstaking, careful way, playing the game over and over, setting the shutter for an automatic click. It probably took hours, an emblem now for all the time they played together.

But then that person, with the strength for such elaborate games, was long since gone.

I don't know how Arden was, not really, because I was, of course, blindsided myself, barely putting one foot in front of the other all the rest of that endless winter, with its long snows and frozen ponds, drifts in the dunes. Maybe it was for the best for Arden, to have a new companion then? Realignment of the pack may be the biggest thing that happens in a dog's life—the rearrangement of social terms, the syntax of the world recast.

Which will be revised again, in seven years' time, when Paul and I bury Beau in the deep sand, in the front garden in Provincetown, under the gravel pathway beside the now-towering forsythia. Arden sits by the side of the grave, lying in his favorite spot in the shelter of the branches—bare, because it's January again—paws crossed in front of him, head down a little, studying what we do: Beau's body wrapped in an Indian bedspread, interred in the ancient way with things he'll need: a tennis ball, biscuits, a special small stuffed toy to carry into the underlife. I keep remembering, who knows why, one afternoon in the park in Iowa City, how Beau'd found a small stuffed animal and lay on his back, keeping it in air with all four paws, with such a look of complete absorption on his face. Michael had been with us that day, with his dog Cowboy, and when he saw Beau's transported face, he caught my eye—a look to say, you see that utter delight, too, don't you? What startles me at the graveside is that he is so beautiful. His illness had swollen his face and his chest with fluids, but that's all gone now; now he looks exactly right: the delicate, ruffled pink of his jowls beneath the plum-colored rubber eraser of the nose.

I'd be lying if I didn't report that there was a side of Arden then that enjoyed being the only dog in the family; no more being jostled aside, no more sharing space or taking turns at the water bowl; had he always wanted to be an only child again? But there's nothing visible of that now; he is motionless, beside the open grave, with his paws crossed before him, his tongue slightly extended, a look on his face I can't begin to read.

Chapter Seven

A walk is a walk and must be taken; breakfast and dinner come when they are due. The routines of the living are inviolable, no hiatus called on account of misery, spiritual crisis, or awful weather. Well, my routines were thoroughly violated; when it came to taking care of myself, I never felt so completely incapacitated. But somehow it was exactly right that I had someone else to take care of. Here was the golden anchor—steady in terms of need if not of behavior. I thought when I brought Beau home I was giving a gift to Wally, but in truth the gift was his to me, or mine to myself, or both. If I'd planned it, I couldn't have done a better thing to save my life.

It wasn't just that he was needy; there was more than that. We'd go out to the Beech Forest, a sheltered tract of woods and dunes that provides a kind of respite, balance to the unboundedness of the high dunes and the immense horizontals of the Atlantic. Beau would race the paths with his paws thundering; he'd lift his head to sniff the wind, taking in all it carried: evidence of snow and, someplace in these woods, a fox; the salt and fish oil tang of the bay. I'd watch him breathing in the world with such delight, and as he did so, his body seemed to be expanding—as if he took the air into his chest, inhaling his new freedom and excitement, and his frame began to flower. There was, indeed, nothing of the saluki about him—maybe a hint of chow, expressed in the genes that splotched his tongue violet—but the body was all golden retriever, slowly growing more muscled, the chest expanding while his shoulders solidified.

"Energy," Blake says, "is eternal delight." Beau's pleasure in the world awakened something in Arden, too. He might well have tumbled into depression just then—had already, I guess, been depressed, in his lazy and heavy months while Wally faded away. Wally'd spent so much time with Arden, they seemed almost of one psychic substance, so attuned to one another's moods. Arden had gained weight from all that bacon-nibbling, curled up most of the day in the big bed while the nurses came and went. "Elizabeth Taylor," Michael called him, the big queen of the comforter.

But now the laconic and contemplative dog—only five years old, after all—had suddenly been called to the life of action. Wally's disappearance was in some way cushioned for him by Beau, if by nothing other than the vast, energetic force of this whirlwind of distraction. They ran together on the paths, Arden panting to keep up, at first, then, once he began to slim down, running with his own dynamic eagerness—though some little catch in his hips wouldn't ever let him be quite as fast, or keep it up for quite so long. Two profiles, one black and one golden, engraved upon my memory, where it is always a winter day, traces of snow marking the paths under a white sky. A frozen pond stretches out ahead of us. We can scuffle our way across that thick ice, which stars beneath our feet in constellations of fissures. One month it was bitter, startlingly cold, and the largest of the ponds was a safe, broad field of ice made tractable by a layer of snow; the wind blew my scarf and their lengthening musk-ox coats while we wandered across a great field the winter had suddenly given us, on our way to hills we'd never find our way to otherwise.

⸱⸱⸱

The phenomenologist Gaston Bachelard writes, "A soul is never deaf to a quality of childhood."

One day in spring, we're walking back from the beach and stop at a yard sale Michael and Frank are having next door. Beau looks over the low table of proffered junk and tchotchkes, extends his neck, and delicately closes his jaws around a purchase of his own—a rubber seagull, with a string attached so you can hang it from the ceiling and let its flexible wings flap. He lifts it gently from the table, closes his teeth more firmly around it, and—lo!—it squeaks. He's thrilled; he makes it squeak again; he tosses it in the air a few inches, catches it, and squeezes it till the faux bird cries. Sold! He carries the prize home, and tosses and bites and slaps till that toy can cry no more.

These outbreaks of puppy behavior can be, despite Bachelard's claim, somewhat less than endearing, though I must admit they seem performed with a certain sly sense of humor. Beau loves, for instance, to steal gloves; he'll get a tricky gleam in his eye, sidle up as if he wants your affectionate attention, and then get his teeth into the fingertips of a glove—done, interestingly, with great delicacy, so as not to injure the hand, just enough pressure to catch the knit of the glove or mitten on those sharp white canines, and then he's off, racing delightedly into the snow with your nicest new striped glove in his jaws, fiercely swinging his head back and forth as if your glove's a mouse whose neck he intends to snap.

And then there's leaping up to grab the leash and walk himself, along with leaping to bite at a sleeve. For some reason, this behavior is especially connected to green things. I like to wear a big green parka I bought to keep Wally warm, and before I know it, there's a rip in the elbow, stuffing starting to fly out. My jade-green rollneck sweater meets a similar fate, the cuff chewed and nibbled—always in fun—till it unravels halfway up my arm. The apotheosis of the green-thing obsession comes with my splashy Benetton apple-green leather gloves—bulky, fleece lined, quite the style, for 1994. They're my favorite, and very warm. We're playing on the harbor beach when Beau snatches one, runs away, turns back toward me as if to laugh. I'm serious this time, I want my glove! He's standing defiantly. I walk closer, closer, I'm reaching down to grab it back—and then he does the one thing that will keep it his. He opens his jaws to a very unlikely width—how does he do that, exactly?—opens the muscles in his throat, breathes in, swallows, and gulp! There goes my very large glove, right down the gullet.

I can't believe it. Is it possible that he could digest it, like a shark? Is whatever they use to dye leather apple green poisonous? Most likely. I keep watch for the afternoon, but he seems fine. I am still contemplating what to do that evening, when Beau begins to look a little bilious, and then—with remarkably little effort, and soon much the better for it—spits up, intact, my now quite undesirable new accessory on the old plank floor.

Walking—a way of being in the present, taking what comes, relinquishing, to some degree, control of what's next, simply following the paths—seems to lift me a little. The beach, the dunes, the Cranberry Bog in Truro, where a long trail through high moors leads to the bluffs over the sea—those are places for warmer days. When it's frigid, the deeper, protected reaches of the woods keep us out of the wind, at least. Beau would take off, catching some scent on the wind, and Arden would bolt after, always trying to catch up, though of course it would be Arden who always came back first. Now and then Beau is gone so long I get worried, but then here he'll come—lifting his ears when he hears his name called, furrowing his brow with curiosity, evidence of attention and focus coming into being. And Arden is gaining a new brightness in the eye, once again that deep, gleaming brown that reminds me of Emily Dickinson describing her own eyes as like "the sherry in the glass that the guest leaves."

Walking is an affirmation of physical life. We're in the world, we're breathing, we're together. I move in a straight line, more or less, along the paths, and sometimes the dogs are right in front of me or beside me, but more often, they are threading around the path, padding in the woods or thickets or marsh on either side of me. I begin to conceive of us as one extended consciousness, reaching out in different directions, sensing, our bodies making a braided trail but our awareness overlapping. That helps, just now, when a self seems fragile, erasable. With the two of them, I'm joined to something else, perception expanded, not just stuck there in the world in my own bereft, perishable, limited body.

It isn't that one wants to live for the sake of a dog, exactly, but that dogs show you why you might want to.

Ethical Fable

*C*athy tells this story: *A man is tired of his dog, doesn't want him, so he takes him out in a boat on a pond, with the intention of drowning the animal. But the boat tips over, and the dog saves the man from drowning.*

I say, "Is that all there is to it?"

"Yes," she says. "It's one of those stories people say is true, and that's all I know about it."

"But," I wonder, "what happened after that?"

This conversation takes place around a breakfast table, and the group lingering over coffee and toast starts trying to imagine what could have been the next part of the story.

Cynthia says, "Of course the man loved the dog then."

I say, "I don't know if people change that much; would a person who could drown a dog really be transformed in that way?"

Robert says, "Now the man will have to find a more efficient way to kill dogs."

I say, "That's so European of you!"

Robert says, "That's so American of you, to say that's European!"

Meredith says, "I think people can be changed by getting shaken up like that. The man could love and honor the dog."

Cathy says, "That's too much of a change. But maybe now he wouldn't drown him."

Robert reconsiders. "You cannot say," he says, "because you don't have enough, how you say it—content?"

Everyone says, "Context!"

"Context, yes," Robert says. "The man might be old and poor, the dog might be sick, the dog might have killed the man's child, you can never say what should be until you know more."

I say, "That really is European!"

Robert says, "Because is why?"

"Because Americans," I tell him, "like things black and white."

I think the man would be changed for a while. Coming close to death like that, I think he could look at the dog and see something—even if he wasn't a very perceptive man—something about their commonality. They have been in the same boat! I don't know if that feeling would last, probably it wouldn't. But for a while, I think he might receive a certain kind of grace, though maybe it's impossible to predict whether people are able to translate grace into action.

I think about this story for days. I ask Paul what he thinks, and he answers, "The man doesn't deserve the dog, he should give the dog to us."

Chapter Eight

I present, to a new boyfriend, a mighty set of challenges, if I do say so myself. I have been a widow(er) for only one year; I am eager to make connection and terrified that anything I love or desire might simply be swept away. I sleep with two seventy-pound retrievers. Paul is undaunted, perhaps because we have known one another in a friendly way for several years; he's sleeping over more of the time, and seems to sort of slide into the house as if he belongs there. Beau, of course, would wiggle his butt and shake his tail cheerfully if Attila the Hun moved in, but Arden has more reservations about the formation of a new arrangement; hasn't he been through enough?

Our energetic coupling clears the bed of beasts. Dogs do not, in my experience, like to be in the same bed, or even the same room, with people having sex—the noise and intensity, the way that intensity can be misread as aggression? But there's usually a dog on the floor nearby, and Paul is not used to waking up in the night and stepping carefully to get to the bathroom. Almost inevitably, he steps on Arden. Each time this takes place, Arden hates it more, until at last, one evening, when Paul jumps out of bed and more or less lands on a black haunch, Arden is off the floor in a flash, teeth bared, furious noises unleashed, and actually chases Paul to the bedroom door with the plain intention of biting him on the butt. This turns out to be a successful strategy; Paul begins, very consciously, to look before he leaps. One battle in the war for dominance has been won.

Another site of contention is the car. Arden's preferred seat is in front, next to me; he thinks Beau should ride in the back. Thanks to our tiny budget, I am, at the time, driving a little mallard-green Toyota, a vehicle into which none of us really fits easily. The first time we all go someplace together, Arden jumps into the front seat, assuming Paul will find a place in the back; the humans are not pleased with this arrangement. If I tell Arden sternly, "Go to the back!" he will, but compliance is accompanied by flattened ears and a dirty look, followed by a sulk. (I use this deep, not-to-be-messed-with voice on very few occasions, usually on the beach when Arden has stolen another dog's ball and some desperate owner is beside herself at the nerve of this recalcitrant beast.) The folk wisdom that stubbornness is the bedfellow of intelligence seems thoroughly demonstrated, since each time we get out of the car, we return to the same scene: Arden in the front passenger's seat, already looking with interest at the journey to come, seemingly nonchalant, and ready to growl the minute Paul makes a motion to displace him.

To growl, and then to wag his tail promptly thereafter, when Paul says, "Shithead," and then begins to love him up.

For, in truth, Arden quite shortly begins to love his Paul, begins to attach to this new person the filaments of his affections. Beau remains cheerfully oblivious.

It's still a lot to ask. One day, I've taken the dogs out to a far marsh when I spy, in the distance, what appears to be a white mattress. A large bit of refuse, for here, but not impossible; the sea can toss up just about anything. The dogs, for some reason, make right for it. I don't know what heaven-sent agency distracts Beau along the way, but Arden will have nothing but that mattress; by the time I get there, he's climbed into the center, flung himself down, and is madly rolling on his back and sides.

I have no way of knowing that the Center for Coastal Studies has performed, just the day before, an autopsy on a beached whale, and that what lies before us is a queen-size mattress of blubber— astonishingly greasy and fishy beyond words, and penetrated now into the depths of Arden's thick and oily coat, where it will remain, only gradually diminishing, for months.

And then there's the skunk. A direct hit, for poor Arden, when he goes out in the driveway at night, right above his eyes. The concentrated spot blooms into an odor of unspeakable intensity. Sitting in the bathtub, basted in tomato juice, he knows he's ridiculous; the plumed tail droops miserably, and the white blazes on his throat and chest are boudoir-pink. More lingering olfactory evidence; Arden is positively symphonic with scent, like that fantasy creation of the decadent symbolist des Esseintes, in Huysmans's nineteenth-century novel, the perfume organ, which sent out into the air a succession of fragrances, calibrated to orchestrate the visions of the dreamer. The pink whorls of his ears, under their lustrous flaps, at least retain the scent they'll carry for all of Arden's life: inexplicably, the nicely sweet odor of corn muffins.

On the other hand, I suppose there's something to be said for joining a pack. We have a sweetness about us, we have a sense of being
a team against or in the face of the world. 1995, in Provincetown,
is a dark hour, and it's a good time to be in this together.

I know I make this sound easy (no story can contain everything). In truth what I felt was deeply dual, one half of my face
turned toward the past and the world I'd lost, the other attendant
to the present and beginning to conceive of a future. As if I am,
myself, black and golden. I don't mean that the personalities of the
dogs in any way represented darkness and light—dogs turn out to
be plenty nuanced, full of dimensions that complicate any easy
definition of character. But their black and gold seemed to me
something more like action versus contemplation, or energy
versus stillness, or fire versus earth. I assigned to them aspects of
myself, as if, when we arrived at the beach and the leashes came
off, those two gestures, one black and one golden, shot out from
my own body.

However much grief I still carried, I liked the way my life was
tending, these bright new directions. It's only human, to mourn
and to reach toward forwardness at once.

I make my living from teaching, mostly, something I couldn't
really do on the Cape, and there were possibilities for guest
appointments in interesting places. So, at the beginning of our first
fall together, Paul and I packed a new station wagon (good-bye,
thank goodness, to the Toyota) with our own necessities and the
necessary animal supplies, leaving enough room in the back for
two large pets to stand, or lie down, or sit and watch half the continent go by, and moved for the semester to Iowa City.

Thus began a peripatetic life of guest semesters here and there, our stints in unfamiliar places punctuated each time by a return to Provincetown for months in between. We are an absurd, single-vehicle caravan, like the Joads making their way out of Oklahoma with pots and pans strapped to the roof, or the Beverly hillbillies hauling Granny's rocker to California. We have computers, books, clothes, water bowls, boxes of biscuits, music for the road, manuscripts in progress, and, of course, the two cats who do not figure in this story riding in their plastic carrying crates and piping up from time to time.

Arden and Beau really are excellent travelers, though Arden is much more likely to let the rocking of the wheels lull him off to sleep. Beau doesn't want to miss anything, especially livestock, and will sit up awake until he looks weirdly bleary-eyed, his head leaning into the window glass. He loves crossing bodies of water, which cause him to stand and stare with consummate alertness, and the aforementioned farm animals, which are greeted with a loud, whooping bark that now and then makes us jump in our seats, when we're not prepared for it.

There are one or two unfortunate livestock-related adventures. Somewhere outside of Buffalo, we pull off the highway at a grassy slope. We're contentedly strolling along when Beau takes off up the hill, and when I get to the top, I can see it's the edge of a loosely fenced pasture. Beau's already in the field, where there are, luckily, no cattle in residence this afternoon. But he does find a large, fresh cow plop, and flings himself into it with abandon. (What is it about smelling horrendous that thrills dogs? The going explanation is that it's a hunting strategy, allowing the wily animal to disguise his own scent with some other. But what good could it possibly do to convince your potential prey that you were an approaching whale, or a moving pile of cow dung?) The cow pile in question is green and unsurpassedly redolent of grass and bovine digestion. We don't have any way to bathe him, so we wipe off what we can, then into the car we go.

Awareness of any smell lasts only a little while, when you're immersed in a cloud of it, but when we pull up to a toll booth on the highway and I roll down the window to pay our two bucks, the attendant herself goes a bit green, and turns away from us as if she's been slapped. Early that evening, in a motel room somewhere upstate, we do some serious violence to the bathtub and the towels.

Motels, in fact, are at the center of our travel life. There's a complete art to it, as we quickly learn; we are two men traveling with four animals and we can't go just anywhere. We tend to the less fancy motels. The newer kind, with a single entrance and a lobby through which all must pass, are out. We look for something a little older, no airs about itself. We pull in at evening, not right in front of the entrance but a bit to the side, so that large canine faces are not immediately visible. If there's not a NO PETS sign, I'll ask, "Do you take dogs?" The usual answer is something like "As long as they're under forty pounds," or "Yes, but there's a twenty-dollar deposit per pet."

I say we have one small dog. This results, invariably, in our being assigned a room in the back of the motel, out of harm's way, where the barking of the alleged miniature creature won't disturb anyone. We pray for a room on the first floor. Perfect. Then, under cover of darkness, the dogs go in first, followed by the not-to-be-narrated cats, water and food bowls, portable cat box, a couple of suitcases, voilà—we're in! Everyone collapses under the air-conditioning. The surprising thing about these evenings is that the dogs seem to love them—each sprawled on a motel bed, after dinner, the AC riffling their coats, they're the image of contented rest. The cats are far less pleased, but our single attempt at sedation produces an awful scene: barbiturate staggering across the motel furniture, grim caterwauling, like some nightmare of drugged starlets on the skids. Now we just try to reassure them and then let them hide under the furniture. Of course, we can't leave, not with this menagerie, so we either have to send out for pizza, or else one of us drives out to see what can be found—which, unsurprisingly, ranges from the merely acceptable to the reprehensible. It's a debased form of travel, no doubt about it. Every morning, we hustle out early, before anybody sees quite how many sentient beings have shared the room for the night. We can't really stop anywhere for long and leave all those creatures in the car. We have many short walks, but we can't stay out long, because the cats must be left behind. So, we wind up just focusing on getting there, the long, unrolling highway, the tires chewing up the miles.

Odd, then, that there's something delightful in the memory, all of us in our icebox of a dumpy motel room, sprawled out on the teal-and-raspberry bedspreads, Paul and I reading or, if we're too tired, letting CNN just scroll by, the dogs so happy to be still they don't move a muscle.

Our first year in Iowa City, we rent a big old house, unfussy, relaxed, with idiosyncratic plumbing and a strikingly long bathtub. It comes with an immensely heavy butcher-block table in the kitchen, to which, we're told, another visiting poet used to tie his unregenerate Rottweiler. One day, a huge maple tree falls in the backyard, victim of one of those ferocious Midwestern thunderstorms; we're lucky it doesn't take our entire household with it. We walk in the afternoons in an extraordinary park—the Hampstead Heath of Iowa City, a poet friend calls it—where mowed grass gives way to woods, and woods to yellow slopes hayed a while ago and now turned to prairie meadows where flocks of deer graze, or do till we draw near. We can lie on our backs in the fields, and watch the huge, white clouds pile up and pass, great tectonic plates of aerial continents.

Our second year in Iowa City, we have a major animal conflict. The school's found us a place to live by following our "one small dog" strategy, and so we wind up way out in Flatview Acres, a dull cul-de-sac of split-levels the color of cream-of-mushroom soup. We rent the home of a professor on sabbatical and his fussy wife. I am not at all comfortable with this deception, but the administrator who takes care of such things at school insists that this is the only way two guys with four pets will ever rent a house anywhere near here, so there seems nothing to do but go along with the ruse.

The landlady leaves pages of instructions and prohibitions, mostly concerning said diminutive pet. Her concerns might be more understandable were the house a trove of, say, delicate antiques, but it's far from it. The furniture's from the local equivalent of IKEA, and the interior—all beige and cream, as though any bit of color would be an unwelcome outburst—is distinguished only by gloomy etchings and a large, spiky wire sculpture of a rat caught on a treadmill. The professor's wife, it seems, did her dissertation on some form of brain research. An entire area of the basement is forbidden to us; we enjoy speculating about what gothic terrors it might contain. A particularly sullen teenage boy, shoulders curved around his narrow chest, appears and mows the lawn. When I go to pay him, he looks like he's not sure he really wants to touch anything that's come from my wallet.

We are totally paranoid, of course, about damaging the vile house, and probably the dogs can sense this, because they seem to become extra destructive, as if our efforts to contain their effects made everyone more nervous and doomed any such plans. One night, a raccoon perches in a tree outside the bedroom window, like an evil sprite sent by the wicked landlady, and the boys go nuts at the window frame. The neighborhood is full of poor, displaced deer, who hang out all night on the trimmed, fertilized lawns; when one wanders by the screen door one afternoon, Beau attempts to go right through it, and more or less does.

Soon we receive word that the suspicious landlady is on her way back to Iowa City from whatever far-flung city she's spending the semester in; she's "forgotten her computer" and plans to drive a dozen hours or so to come get it. We go into action. All evidence of animals is squirreled away, mostly into the car. Cats go into crates, dogs into the back of the wagon, and we're off for the day. Just to escape, we drive to Wisconsin, which turns out to be rather pleasant, and, to my delight, we discover the Dickeyville Grotto, a monument of outsider art built in the early years of the century by an exiled Alsatian priest who longed for the baroque architecture of home, and so decided to make some out of whatever was at hand. It's a temple of idiosyncrasy, just the kind of art I like, and we'd never have found it if we weren't on the lam.

We are, however, caught. One day, when we're not home, the owners' daughter appears, and promptly reports to her mother that all four of our animals were perched together, napping on the white living-room couch. This is plainly an untruth; the cats wouldn't go anywhere *near* those dogs, much less sleep with them, and the wobbly modular couch would slide around hopelessly anyway, if any pet tried to jump up on it. But it does make for a dramatic vision to strike horror into a mother's heart.

Recriminations, accusations. We come clean. I have a terrific fight at work with the woman who made the housing arrangements, a shouting match of startling proportions, in which she cries out, "Mark, I don't care if you sleep on the fucking street!" She is having a very bad day, but so much for the vaunted privilege of academe. The owners of the house do not sue us or send us any startling bills, but I suspect it's for a sad and disturbing reason. Just before we go, we get a death threat on our answering machine, clearly left by one of the neighbor boys—that same sour boy who'd come to mow the lawn? "Queer I'm gonna kill you," he says. Which seems to be enough, for the owners of the house, to put things in a bit of perspective. We are delighted to leave their neighborhood behind, and, of course, the dogs are happy to get in the car to go anywhere.

Even in the awful suburbs, there were long walks in the forest nearby, while the leaves turned every imaginable shade of yellow, and deer stirred in the oak groves near twilight, stepping high on their weirdly delicate legs. Beau would disappear on one of his vast, looping runs, and, in a while, come bounding up the railroad ties that shaped the rustic steps, tongue askew, radiating pleasure in his own speed. Then we'd walk the grassy shoulder of the road to the CreeMee stand, with its painted, wooden ice-cream cone towering into the bluing air, and both dogs would wait patiently to finish my cone.

In a borrowed house in the woods in Vermont, one summer, Paul plays the piano especially for Beau, who comes and lies down on the braided rug beside the bench, stretches out to his full length, and lets the music vibrate down the length of him. Liturgical music, Joni Mitchell, bits of show tunes, Laura Nyro—Beau goes straight to the piano whenever Paul begins to play, and takes in any genre equal delight.

Our first year in Salt Lake, we discover the Benches, the scrubby foothills of the mountains that ring two sides of the town. We live in a high, Victorian neighborhood near the university (the only place in town where the cars sport bumper stickers like LOVE YOUR MOTHER or THANK GODDESS), so the Benches are minutes away, by car, and startlingly wild. Mule deer trot above us on rocky bluffs; we mount a crest, and a coyote lopes off, looking back over his shoulder. Beau tries to follow, running full tilt on the scratch of a hiking path that winds up the side of the mountain, but he's no match for his wild cousin who runs those slopes every day of his life.

One day, the four of us are high up on the bench-side—the foothills of the Wasatch Range—when we are stopped in our tracks by something large, dark, stirring in a small thicket up ahead. We move a little closer, and it dawns on Paul and me at once that this ungainly-looking thing, taller than a refrigerator, as wide as four refrigerators lined up, is a moose. A female, antlerless moose, contentedly consuming a small tree. She tears a branch from the trunk, she chews, seems to consider, chooses another; she doesn't move from the neck down.

I don't have to do a thing to control the dogs; they both sit down as if commanded to do so, lean their heads forward, and watch as if this particular spectacle is one not to be missed.

The Beau I first encountered would have run right up to that moose, immensity or no; his reserved, appropriate contemplation of the beast is evidence of the way he's changed. In Provincetown, he used to swim after seals, who seemed very curious about their terrestrial cousins but also quite willing to keep swimming out farther and farther as Beau followed them along, till eventually he'd be just a dark speck in the distance, out in the winter sea. We'd be horrified, and more than once we were sure we'd lost him—and then he'd come running down the beach from wherever the current had pulled him, shivering, practically blue in the cold. The child, we used to say, is without limits.

But now our joke is that he's grown a neocortex, his brain evolved through a combination of love, exercise, fresh air, and an excellent brand of canned food called Triumph. He and Paul have connected during some times I've been away, in a way they couldn't conjoin before, back when Beau was just wiggly attention to whatever bright stimulus appeared at the moment. There's something thoughtful about him now; new qualities have emerged that we'd never really have expected: a dignity and poise, even an aspect of nobility. When he swims in the Great Salt Lake, water so thick with salinity it's weirdly buoying, he rides up high on the small waves, his mouth closed, his dignified head sailing above the surface.

Physically, he's at his most strapping, big and bright. One day, a photographer comes to the house, to take some pictures for a literary publication; she snaps a shot of me at my desk, my eyebrows raised in the middle of making a joke. I'm never especially photogenic, but Beau looks like a radiant flare of solar well-being, standing at the foot of my desk, occupying a good half of my tiny study. The picture's published in a book of postcard photos of poets. It's a completely reassuring joy, six months later, when I'm far from home, in Ireland, missing the steady domestic supports of my life, and I walk into a bookstore in Galway and there, pinned to the wall, is that postcard of me and my shining friend.

Being away, of course, necessitates that we find dog-sitters. There is no better profession than mine for one who seeks people interested in such work: graduate students are often far from home and from beloved animals, and often living in spartan conditions. Thus, asked if they'd like to spend a week in a comfortable house, with lots of good books, cable TV, and a stereo—and oh, four pets—they're often delighted. When I have a class over to the house, I confess, I keep an eye out for a student who especially gravitates to the dogs.

In this way, Arden and Beau made particularly splendid friends, and engraved themselves upon the imaginations of a number of young writers. Nuar took the dogs jogging along the beach, even managing to wear *them* out in the salty tide flats. Karen walked the deep trails by the Coralville Reservoir, down to the muddy red water, and cooked dinner for young poets while the dogs delighted in the company. Jenn read in bed in Provincetown, one dog sprawled on either side of the covers beside her, one head on each of her thighs. Julie, a former Alaskan dog-musher who once nearly froze to death on the back of a sled—and who reported that the rumor about freezing being pleasurable, even transcendent, seems to be entirely true—took them hiking in fields of sunflowers deep in the Wasatch.

From time to time, though it's no one's preference, a kennel is a necessity. The strangest of these, on Stock Island, near Key West, was run by an old woman named Mae, who sat in her front room in a flowered housedress and said in a voice shredded by decades of Chesterfields, "They'll be fine," with absolutely no affect, as though she'd said it a thousand times. I look doubtful. She says, "What's a matter? A night away from home won't hurt 'em none." Her services are alarmingly inexpensive. Her little stucco house is painted a peeling tropical green that might once have been lime, and there are stucco kennel-houses beside it, and, frankly, it seems like some kind of strange Haitian voodoo catacomb—but we don't know anyone here, and must both be in Miami overnight, and there *are* other dogs around, so somebody trusts her. A little gravel yard is marked by a withering, defeated elephant's ear. Am I just being a snob? This is the funkiest outpost of Florida life I've ever seen, but there's no actual sign of trouble; it's just that everything, Mae included, feels right on the edge of ruin, as if it'll tumble into a swamp without a trace of its ever having been. The place smells of cold concrete and vegetation and, what? Cantaloupe?

We are completely nervous about Mae's kennel all our twenty-four hours in the sleek, couldn't-be-farther-from-Mae world of South Beach. We go straight from the Key West airport to Mae's, where we're greeted with the same response we get any time we return: both dogs leap in the air in a way that seems unlikely if not impossible: standing up on their hind legs, they lift off, make exuberant twisting shapes in the air, land on all fours, then do it again. Completely none the worse for wear.

⁓

It's so hot in Houston when we arrive in August, so ferociously humid, that walking under the big live oak trees—with their thick arms that curve out low over the sidewalk and the street, and their roots that buckle the pavement into steep angles and declivities—is only possible in the early morning and evening, but even then we're slapping at tiny mosquitoes that deliver a wickedly pointed sting. Soon we're told about the dog park, a green belt beside Buffalo Bayou (in which, it's rumored, urban alligators lie in wait, down there with discarded box springs and trash and Lord knows what. It's said that a disgruntled letter-carrier has been tossing mail in there for years). There, in a wide, safe bowl of grass, dogs get off leash to play.

Best of all, there's a fountain—one of those splashy models that resembles, when the jets are on, a dandelion head gone to seed. It's a marvel—in the air is a great, cool spray of water, the wind, when there is any, blowing a delicate spray of mist all over everyone, and below it a pond full of dogs of all shapes and colors, cooling. Arden, who's nearly ten, is just arthritic enough now that he can't quite make it over the rim on his own, most of the time, but once he's in the water, he stands there, under a spray of liquid cool, letting himself get soaked all the way to the skin. Beau prefers walking in a circle around the fountain, or chasing a ball, though after a spate of running and leaping into the fountain, he also just likes to stand, immobile, while the more restless leapers and wrestlers flash all around him.

There's an overpass beside the park, and when we walk on the footpath beneath it, there's an odd, acrid scent—the urine of generations of bats, who cleave to the concrete beams above. At a particular twilight hour, they wake and rise, in a steady, flittering stream, moving past the fountain, along the perimeter of the trees, down toward the bayou. We've run, Arden and Beau and I, on the path beneath them, that stream of small, twittering life above our heads, their motion making a kind of music in the dusk. They make me think *of A Midsummer Night's Dream*, Oberon's legions, the spirits of the woodland wending their braided, airy path into the night—in the middle of the office towers of Houston.

In this way, while we're considering where to live, how to find or make a home for ourselves, five years pass.

Ordinary Happiness

*W*e're pulling up to a drive-in bank teller's window. Mr. Beau's in the backseat, head out the driver's-side window, and the weary teller lights up as soon as she sees him, for as soon as Beau spies a human face, he lets loose a radiant flurry of greeting—grinning, tongue lolling, tail wagging so intensely that the rear half of his body switches from side to side. It's as if he's known the woman all his life, though he's never laid eyes on her. She produces a small biscuit, which is passed through the metal drawer that extends mechanically from her containing space into my containing space. She watches him gulp it down, then she says, "Their work is just to bring joy into this world."

Chapter Nine

I'm worried about the fatty lump under Arden's left leg, right where it joins his torso. Labs get these all the time, and while they're unappealing, they aren't dangerous. But this one's awkwardly positioned, maybe contributing to his trouble with his hips. He seems to be perfectly cheerful and in a resoundingly good mood, but it doesn't seem like a good idea to sport a lump the size of an orange. So, we're looking for a new vet in Houston, and how we find Tandy Tupper (this is Texas, after all, and names have a different music than they do in the north) I cannot recall. She has an outrageously busy office, where it is very difficult to get her or anyone else's attention, and once you do get five minutes of her time, her preferred method of operation is to fill you with alarm. Tandy Tupper has hair piled high and loose, lots of Native American–looking bangles, and a pleasant manner that shifts quickly into a heightened state of alarm when she senses a crisis to be met. Yes, Arden's lump is so large that it could grow into the muscle under his haunch, yes, it must go. He'll need first to fast, and then have some tests, to make sure he's a good candidate for surgery.

Days later, disgruntled at not being fed for twelve hours, Arden is trundled off to Dr. Tupper just after dawn, only to wait in a huge line of pets seeking attention. There's a backup in surgery, crises abounding, and it's late in the afternoon before we hear that Arden has been found an unsuitable candidate for anesthesia: his heart has a funny wobble to it, and his liver is shrunken. What this means is left vague, though it seems his death rattle may be imminent. We're instructed there's nothing to do but further tests, which, she cautions us, may well prove inconclusive, but Tandy recommends a visit to the state-of-the-art animal medical center, where it takes months to get an appointment. The other option, she mentions in passing, is to keep an eye on him and hope for the best.

＊

Emily Dickinson says that hope, *that thing with feathers—That perches in the soul,* cannot be silenced; *it never stops—at all—*But because she is a great poet, in a little while she will say a completely contradictory thing. She who *felt a funeral* in her brain, the underlying planks of sense giving way, most certainly understood depression and despair. Perhaps even in her famous poem figuring hope as a bird, she hints at the possibility of hope's absence, since if hope has feathers, it is most likely capable of flying away.

Paul has a bracingly Slavic attitude toward hope. His ancestors starved in the fields outside of Bratislava, between plagues and invasions, and their notion that hoping for a better future would have been a costly act of self-delusion seems practically written into his genes. He would agree with Virgil, who says in his *Georgics*, "All things by nature are ready to get worse."

But this is ultimately something of a pose, a psychic costume for a sensibility no less vulnerable than my own. He believes that low expectations about the future will protect him—whereas I, six years older and thus a child of the sixties, can't stop myself from thinking, perhaps magically, that our expectations shape what's to come.

Though it's true that I, who am more likely to hope overtly, publicly, am also more likely to crash the harder when that hope is voided.

≈

Back in Provincetown, we see our old vet, and Arden's body is declared quirky but workable. Both dogs test positive for exposure to Lyme disease, though—the consequence of all those years of walking the brushy trails of the Cape. The implications of the test results seem murky; being exposed to the disease doesn't mean you have it. Arden's antibody count is so low that the diagnosis is in doubt, but Beau's definitely a candidate for a course of antibiotics. Has he been a bit less energetic, is his coat a little bit oily? It's hard to be sure. The first pill we try—fat tablets wrapped up in a slice of cheese—makes him woozy; if he were a cartoon dog, he'd have little X's for eyes and some wavy lines floating around his head. Antibiotic number two doesn't seem to bother him a bit.

Back in Houston, time for an annual checkup. Tandy T. declares that Arden may well be perishing before our eyes, though he's doing so quite slowly. But then she puts Beau on the scale, finds he's lost six pounds since last year, and has this intuition something's not right, not Lyme disease this time, something else.

I know it's true, and little pieces of evidence suddenly seem to have meaning. Doesn't he stand in the spraying water of the dog fountain a bit longer, not moving at all? And once, as he was standing by the kitchen door, waiting for his dinner, didn't one of his hind legs step backward, in a little twitch that looked—well, not right. Of course it's true—I know it in the way you know things, once they are named, that have been right under your nose all along, visible but not really acknowledged—as much because they are frightening as because they are not named. He's not the same dog. He lies in the dining room, all sprawled out, or with his head stretched out on the floor, chin flat in front of him, in a way that conveys listlessness. He greets and thumps his tail but he doesn't leap up, and even his thumping seems of briefer duration.

But the general bedlam of the very popular Dr. Tupper's office and that dire-crisis mentality make me feel that this is not the place to figure out what's up. She hasn't exactly gotten anywhere with Arden, though he's exasperatedly fasted and we've spent hours upon hours waiting to get him into surgery. That's how, through one of my student's enthusiastic recommendations, we come to Dr. Frank.

His office is a calmer, much less fancy place in an unpretentious neighborhood. The Hispanic woman behind the desk has pictures of her kids taped to her computer; all over the walls are letters and cards from people thanking Frank for taking care of their cats and birds, lizards and snakes and dogs. The place has a nice multiracial mix, a good-spiritedness, people calmly going about their business.

Frank himself has slicked-back hair and horn-rimmed glasses; he's lean, energetic, and somewhat awkward. He gives the impression of one who probably isn't socially confident or authoritative in arenas other than this one. In the office, he's commanding, engaged, and he gives his numerous assistants orders with the firm demeanor of a surgeon in a TV show—save that, one senses, there's affection all-around for him, despite, perhaps, a bit of eye-rolling about the extremely specific way in which he expects things to be done. Animals are carried in *this* way; a needed tool is provided from *this* side; alertness is always required—no daydreaming! His assistant—clearly new—a soft-featured, muscled man with many tattoos, wears his blue scrubs like a prison uniform and never utters a word.

Frank notices the texture of Beau's coat—the way it leaves a slight shiny residue on your hands—and the way you can grab a good-size handful of skin on his back and pluck it up away from the muscles: evidence of dehydration. Dr. Frank already has a theory, and the blood work shows he's right: Beau has kidney disease, which means his body can't adequately process the protein in his diet, which means his health is failing.

There isn't a cure, but there are things to do. Primarily, a low-protein diet—rice with, say, a tiny bit of chicken to make it tempting, that kind of thing. If the protein's lowered, Frank says, then his kidneys can last longer, hard to say how much.

But, first, a night in the hospital, getting filled up with fluids intravenously to replace those he's lost and get him hydrated. Beau trots off with the tattooed attendant, quite pleased to be going, not at all aware that we aren't coming along. Then he turns back to look, understands that I am not coming, and starts to bolt back to me. I scratch his ears and his beautiful rump, about to let him go. But Frank is perfectly happy to let me walk with him back into the hospital room, where the patients go but the clients usually don't. I can say good-bye to him there, and hand him over to the attendant—who is, I can tell, already smitten with him.

Beau comes back looking a whole lot better. It isn't until I see him the next morning in Frank's waiting room, enlarged, shining with all the water he's taken in, that I understand just how much he's faded. When we see those things happen gradually, of course, day by day, it's hard to measure how far they've gone. Paul and I have been speaking as if there were hope, because it seemed necessary for us to do so together, as if to name what we both felt, beneath the surface, were too dangerous—would make his dire condition too real, solidify it in words.

But now we're startled at how great he looks, and the hope that we have steeled ourselves against feeling begins to stir.

We begin the dietary regime, which involves boiling up large quantities of rice to keep in the refrigerator and commingle, at mealtime, with various temptations. There's a specially formulated canned dog food you can buy, too, but it has a density and weight that suggest some kind of modeling compound, and we never succeed in convincing Beau that there's much about it to like. We are regular visitors to Frank's, for blood work, and it's soon plain that Beau is the most popular dog in the clinic. He is welcomed by everyone, affectionately greeted, and even walks from room to room without a lead; when someone says, "Come with me," he trots behind, and seems cheerfully to allow the necessary procedures, as if proud of himself and devoted to maintaining his reputation.

Still that funny tremble in one hind leg, now and then.

Frank puts him on a round of steroids, injections that will start to replace some of the muscle he's lost. We joke that Beau's becoming a Chelsea boy, ready for a circuit party. Over the course of a week or ten days, we can see that they're working: Beau begins to move with a bit more energy, to seem more like his old self, to Frank's delight. It's then I understand that he's an artist; this is what he makes, animals in better shape, human happiness. Whenever I go to see Frank, he tells me a story—a beaten and abandoned dog he's taken in, pro bono, a bird who dropped dead on his watch, his first month out of vet school. His work is, as well as medical, narrative; he's weaving a set of tales, stories of education and restoration.

Frank has been literally weaving some stories, as well; he reveals, in one of our conversations, when he finds out that I'm a writer and a teacher, that he's written a novel, a detective story featuring a sleuthing vet. I'm so grateful for what he's done for Beau, and for the sweet, steady attention we've received from all of Frank's crew, that I volunteer to read it.

The book's about a small-town vet, who punctuates his reports on tracking down a murderer with chapters recounting particular encounters with particular pets. There's that undiagnosable bird, and recalcitrant cats, and dogs of great heart and persistence; the vet stories are delightful and unmistakably real; the detective part is—well, not my cup of tea. I bring the manuscript back to Frank with encouragement, and he confesses that the murder bit is just there to get the reader interested. I tell him where he can sign up for a memoir class, and he's boyishly delighted at the idea that I really think he ought to.

One of the things that being a vet is about is the continual restoration of hope, bringing back the possibility of companionship, making a stage upon which love may continue.

Can hope really be in vain, can you be harmed by hope? Obviously, there is hope that amounts to nothing, in terms of the wished-for result, the longed-for cure, the desired aim. But is that hope in vain, is it simply lost? Or can we say that there's some way it makes a contribution to the soul—as if one had been given some internal version of those steroid shots, a dose of strengthening?

Hope is leaven; it makes things rise without effort. I have moved forward at times without hope, when Wally was sick and dying, and there wasn't a thing in the world to do but ease his way. Without hope, you hunker down and do what needs to be done in this hour; you do not attend to next week. It is somehow like writing without any expectation or belief that one will ever be read—only worse, since even a Dickinson secreting her poems away in private folios sewn by hand expects, at some unknowable time, her treasure to be found, her words to be read. Hopelessness means you do the work at hand without looking for a future.

Beginning to believe that Beau could be . . . not healed, but live well a good while, that's a good thing, isn't it, that gesture of belief? It doesn't hurt him, our trying, and there was that burst of gain that made Paul and me feel, well, he could . . .

And it's as if Beau feels it, too, especially one day in the dog park. Lately, he sits and watches, where he used to energetically chase after tennis balls, or run in some temporary pack. Gradually, he hasn't trusted himself in the group, unable to rely on his old strength, and more of the time he's just been a watcher at the rim. But one day, after the steroid shots, he moves forward with interest when someone throws a ball, and then, instead of allowing the impulse to fade away, he instead hurtles forward, an amazing burst of energy and speed, a surprised look on his face, as if he didn't know he could still do it, as if he himself has filled with hope, having found his body can still fly.

So different from what I see, in a few weeks' time, when we're on our way to New York. A visiting appointment at NYU brings with it a large apartment in the Village, and they even let us have dogs there. We go home to Provincetown for a few weeks on the way, for December in our old, beloved house, the lights stringing the tower of the Monument down the hill, wind off the bay, a dose of cold New England Christmas. I'm alone with the dogs in woods we know well, paths winding through beech and oak groves and outcrops of dune, and we turn to hike up a familiar hill—a slope Beau would have gone racing up, last year. He begins, as if his body leads the way, and suddenly there's a hesitation, and he stops, his shoulders lowering back down out of the anticipated sprint upward in what appears to be a sort of sigh of resignation, a relinquishment. The hill is too much. We take a low path toward home.

Old Photo

*H*ere's a photo taken years ago: Arden and Beau, running up Pearl, our Provincetown street where we've lived all these years. I don't remember taking this picture, but I must have been standing at the bottom of the street, close to the bay; up the snowy slope of the hill, the two rumps of the dogs, their two plumed tails in the air, one black and one golden. Pearl Street curves up from the harbor; the story goes that the curve is because in the old days, when wheelbarrows were pushed up the hill full of dried salt cod, it was easier to make it up the low dune there if you didn't try to go straight uphill. Now that curve is made permanent, and lined with houses that have seen, over our fifteen years here, wild changes. Here was where Billy lived, and here the elderly widow of a painter; here was the guesthouse Hans ran, living in devotion and thrall to his Turkish boyfriend, who'd take the bus to go window-shopping in Hyannis, and dismount again exclaiming about the beautiful jewels he'd seen in the stores there at the mall. Here lived Franco, who in the last years of his life converted part of his apartment into a gallery selling art deco objets d'art. Here lived Antony, in my favorite house, a narrow little Dutch gambrel whose shingles were overtaken by moss. Antony had been born there, and lived out his days in that tiny place, repairing violins and caring for a succession of springer spaniels. By the time I knew him, he was ancient, though no one could seem as old as his spectacularly moth-eaten spaniel, with his matted tangle of fur, who liked to lie in the yard like a heap of ruined tapestry. Antony seemed matted himself; the same army woolens winter and summer. He was entirely deaf but loved to talk to anyone who'd listen. The story went that his mother was deeply devoted to scrubbing and the cleanliness of the body, and that upon her death, Antony renounced all such practices forever. When her washing machine fell through the weary floor of his little house, there in the cellar it remained.

Now Antony's house has been gutted and sheetrocked and equipped with recessed lighting and a huge new window to accommodate the view; the mossy shingles have been hauled to the dump—just as the last of Antony's dogs and then Antony himself were also hauled away—and the new shingles shine with a sort of chocolatey-plum varnish. The whole thing gleams like a vaguely dangerous piece of pastry. It has a koi pond and a fountain. Billy's old place is outfitted for groups of sleek summer renters from Boston and New York, who throw parties that spill out through the new French doors onto the stairs. Hans's old guesthouse was dormered, renamed, decked, and painted aqua blue. Later, sold again, it's coated a strident shade of red. Of Franco's retail experiment, there remained for several years an odd little lamp beside his old shop door marked with a thirtiesish design that would have held no meaning if you didn't know what it had illuminated— but now that's gone, too.

I hate the wild reinventions of time on my street, and I try to remember that they were, of course, going on long before I got there, and that I myself took an old house—once lavender, with a few straggly irises out front—and remade it in my image of what an old house on the Cape ought to be. I planted roses where some flintier soul was *content with grass. The physical reinvention of the world is endless, relentless, fascinating, exhaustive; nothing that seems solid is. If you could stand at just a little distance in time, how fluid and shape-shifting physical reality would be, everything hurrying into some other form, even concrete, even stone.*

But in the photo, my two princes are still loping up the street, walking in step, as they often did, in the early winter darkness that's just beginning to deepen, headed through a snow which has stilled any traffic and muffled the town, so that there's no sound but a little wind and wave-lapping, and the chink of some beached boat's chain, and the footfalls of dogs headed toward a towel-drying, to wipe away the melted snow that's chilled their coats, toward dinner and then the long ritual of licking paws, cleaning away the residue of damp, and then sleep, in a warm house, while the enveloping night comes on.

Chapter Ten

How can you hide, wrote Heraclitus, from what never goes away?

Death is always present—peeking out of the pocket, down in the socket of the bone, the shadow in the photograph, the fleck in the iris of a living eye, deep blue underside of the wave. Never out of sight, only out of mind, and how do we learn to live with such corrosive pressure? Every time I think I know, death laughs at me and pulls the dark hat a little lower over my eyes, takes one of my hands and leads me firmly toward what I am to see: reminders, evidence, memento mori. *Vanitas*. The bubble breaks, the taper's extinguished, the eye sockets of the skull fill with a darkness scented with that spent candle's smoke.

I had a dream, when I was young, which I have never forgotten. I'd gone to a meditation retreat in the desert mountains outside of Tucson with a friend. We were sixteen or seventeen, and thrilled with the possibilities of transcendence. (This is ironic, in retrospect; we didn't know enough of the world to want to rise above it. What we wanted to transcend, I think, was adolescence.) We believed the meditative technique we practiced would, as our teacher said, lead us painlessly and directly toward the gates of enlightenment, though with plenty of time for adventure along the way.

At the retreat, we spent our evenings listening to taped lectures from India, and asking questions of the teachers who were there with us in the flesh. Then we'd have a group meditation session where someone would often get the giggles, passed down the line in contagious waves; one night, a girl in front of me dissolved in laughter that I could feel breaking over me in lovely, silly waves. She turned around to me, still laughing, tears in her eyes. "Sorry," she said, "it must be that last acid trip ... ," and then the two of us just laughed all the harder. This happened, our instructor said, because someone was releasing some heavy, internalized stress. By day, we practiced round after round of yoga, breathing exercises, and sessions of meditation. After a few of these rounds, I'd be so blissed out I'd simply drift away to sleep. I'd feel deep and clear as a well; a stone dropped into me might fall for the longest time.

But this dream came to me, one afternoon, with the kind of hallucinatory gravity and clarity only a few dreams in a lifetime possess. I was in a rowboat on a flat, wide expanse of sea, beneath an immense sky where white clouds towered; the rowboat was moving slowly, inexorably, rowed by a skeleton who kept a steady pace. I began to look directly at my ferryman's face, or the place where his face had been. My point of view—I was a camera eye now—came closer and closer to the skull, which seemed huge, the size of one of those grand, billowing clouds, and when I looked into the dark sockets of those eyes, I was suddenly utterly and completely terrified, because I saw through those holes only the great expanse of the sky; there was nothing there, behind that blank, but the great open emptiness of the world. I woke up screaming. I startled my friend, who came running into the room to see if I was all right. I told him my dream. "Man," he said, "you're really releasing some stress."

≈≈

I wonder now if that dream came to me as a kind of corrective, a balancing vision to weigh against the rather unqualified affirmation our meditation classes suggested; simply release all your stress, through the regular practice of the mantra, our teachers encouraged, and you'll arrive at unity, completeness, bliss. Maybe so. But the great looming skull had another thing to say. What you are, it seemed to insist, is air; beneath the solid self lie the bones, and beneath the bones simply the clean, whistling, open void. It's the other pole of life, the negation that lives beneath the yes; the fierce chilly gust of silence that lies at the core of music, the hard precision of the skull beneath the lover's face. The cold little metallic bit of winter in the mouth. One is not complete, it seems, without a taste of that darkness; the self lacks gravity without the downward pull of the void, the barren ground, the empty field from which being springs.

But then, the problem of the depressive isn't the absence of that gravity, it's the inability to see—and, eventually, to feel—anything else. Each loss seems to add a kind of weight to the body, as if we wore a sort of body harness into which the exigencies of circumstance slip first one weight and then another: my mother, my lover, this house, that garden, a town as I knew it, my own fresh and hopeful aspect in the mirror, a beloved teacher, a chestnut tree in the courtyard of the Universalist Meeting House. They are not, of course, of equal weight; there are losses at home and losses that occur at some distance; their weight is not rationally apportioned.

My grandfather, whom I loathed, weighs less to me in death than does, I am embarrassed to admit, my first real garden, which was hard-won, scratched out of Vermont soil thick with chunks of granite, and a kind of initial proof of the possibility of what love could make, just what sort of blossoming the work of home-keeping might engender. Sometimes I seem to clank with my appended losses, as if I wear an ill-fitting, grievous suit of armor.

There was a time when such weight was strengthening; it kept me from being *too* light on my feet; carting it about and managing to function at once required the development of muscle, of new strength. But there is a point at which the suit becomes an encumbrance, something that keeps one from scaling stairs or leaping to greet a friend; one becomes increasingly conscious of the plain fact of heaviness.

And then, at some point, there is the thing, the dreadful thing, which might, in fact, be the smallest of losses: of a particular sort of hope, of the belief that one might, in some fundamental way, *change.* Of the belief that a new place or a new job will freshen one's spirit; of the belief that the new work you're doing is the best work, the most alive and true. And that loss, whatever it is, its power determined not by its particular awfulness but merely by its placement in the sequence of losses that any life is, becomes the one that makes the weighted suit untenable. It's the final piece of the suit of armor, the plate clamped over the face, the helmet through which one can hardly see the daylight, nor catch a full breath of air.

⟨⟩

How to deal with the blank at the back of the skull I saw when I was sixteen?

The Tibetan Buddhists have a solution of sorts, or at least what suggests to me a solution: a sky funeral. On the most material level, it's a way of dealing with the problem of burying the dead in a stony, frozen landscape where digging's more or less out of the question. This is how it works: when a person dies, after the vigil is kept over the body, and prayers are said to smooth the way of the soul on its transition between worlds, then it's time to dispose of the flesh. There are men called *tomden*, who have the specific task—nothing for the fainthearted—of doing the work. The corpse is taken to a rocky slope set aside for this purpose, and there a juniper fire is built to signal the birds. The *tomden*, a sort of spiritual butcher, unwraps the body and slices it open to the bone. All the time the vultures have been gathering and watching, for they have centuries—millennia?—of memories. They descend. "Eat, eat," cries the *tomden*, and in no time at all the flesh is gone. The *tomden* walks in among the vultures and takes the skeleton apart, tossing bones to the birds; then, with a stone sledgehammer, he breaks whatever bones remain. He crushes the skull, mixes the fragments with flour, and calls to the birds again, and in a little while, the body's gone, absolutely and utterly. Where there was the physical fact of a person, now there are wings, air, flight, the noise and hurry of passage. It is a statement of enormous power. That the body is almost nothing at all—evanescent, consumable. That the body returns to the world, given back. That the appropriate response to death might, in fact, be a kind of abandon: let whatever was quick and animating in us fly free, and throw whatever remains to the winds, to the fires of hunger, to the engines of appetite.

That's all the body is worth, throw it away!

Could we import such an attitude toward loss? Of course, everything perishes, we might say, why not? I, you, our beloveds, our aspirations, our possessions, they all vanish, so, throw them loose, relinquish, move forward boldly in this moment of the world, this arena of flesh.

Everything dies, because the world's only a constantly mutating mask for the deep, wild life of energy, veiling itself over and over as matter, taking shape in order to express the dynamic nature of its character, plunging into matter and sailing up—as if inside the belly of a vulture—into energetic life again.

Isn't this a bracing sort of negation? Ah, throw it all to hell and gone, of course we'll die. So now what?

≈≋

The opposite approach to the radical detachment of sky burial is to hold on with all one's might to the world. I think probably most of us go back and forth along a continuum between these two approaches—attachment and relinquishment, energetic movement and the stasis of the firm grasp. These have been the two poles of my life: to be, on the one hand, absolutely without control, like a piece of straw floating on the waters of time and of contingency. And, on the other, to attempt with all my power to hold on, to refuse loss, to try not to admit death and decay, to make any stays that I could against the current. That's what it is to be human, isn't it? Connected and always about to disconnect, bound and free, burdened and weightless. A sense of immensity balanced by a nearly unbreakable link to the intimate.

This condition of polarity, of irreconcilable points of view, is contained in a little poem—only five short lines, but with worlds in it!—by a Japanese warrior, Fuse Yajiro. It was written in the month before his death.

Seen from
outside creation
earth and sky
aren't worth
a box of matches.

Yajiro has the bracing detachment of a sky burial; what could be more ephemeral, more easily replaceable than a box of matches? But the first two lines of the poem are crucial: this is the perspective of one who's already left the world, who stands outside looking in. And, of course, the truth is that Yajiro's poem was written by a living man, not a dead one; he may already be seeing his way back to earth from the cool realms of space, but he's still here, embodied, still capable of putting ink to a page. Therefore his vision extends from the infinite—the cool reaches of the void—to the infinitesimal: the ordinary little physical fact of a book of matches.

Here *inside* the world, of course, earth and sky are everything, and, in truth, for a cold man, or someone dying for a cigarette, a box of matches might be precious indeed. The point is that Fuse Yajiro lives, in his last month of breath, in two places at once, on two planes. Perhaps this paradox has simply been sharpened by the advent of his ending; maybe this dual perspective is where he's *always* lived. How can we do otherwise but to love the world, and also understand that it's merely a concatenation of dust and sparks?

But I lost sight of this, and thus found my way toward an alternative means of dealing with that stubborn blank darkness: I became ill. After years and years of resisting, of reaching toward affirmation, of figuring that there must always be a findable path, a possible means of negotiating against despair, my heart failed. Or, to change the metaphor, we could say what quit was my nerve, or my pluck, or my tenacity, or my capacity for self-deception. I was coming toward a zero, and this is how I got there.

Zero Point

*T*he worst moment of my life happened on the Staten Island Ferry. Nobody knew. It was entirely invisible, taking place on an internal level, beneath the surface, and it terrified me so completely I didn't talk about it at all, even to Paul.

January 2001, we've been in New York a few weeks, and we take the dogs to Sandy Hook in the car for an outing. Sandy Hook's an undeveloped promontory on the Jersey Shore which pokes up toward New York Harbor, a beautiful, wild place of dunes and scrubby, coastal forests. The trails are snowy at the edges, the air sharp with salt, ice, and pine, and the dogs love it.

Every day we've been performing our afternoon ritual: Beau and I go off into the bedroom and sit quietly, and in a bit I jab the skin between his shoulder blades somewhere with a needle, and let as much of a sac of clear fluid as I can drip down under his skin, nourishing his body. It's become a sort of meditation time; it's awful, but I try to make of it a stillness for him, a companionable half an hour. Still, he seems weak and tired. Arden's a bit startled as well, finding himself in New York City. Every day we take the elevator down to the lobby, stroll north toward Washington Square, and enter the surprising arena of the dog park, a location of fascination for the dogs but, *doubtless, some tension, too—a little too much for them now, all that jostle and rowdy life?*

Whatever the case, they love Sandy Hook. They are running the trails, sniffing in the snow, rolling. It seems like the old days, sprightly dogs sporting in the cold. When we get to the beach, Beau finds a trove of clam shells—the big, empty casings of sea clams—and begins to gnaw on them with abandon, crunching them up in his teeth. Is there some mineral in there he's craving? They're worn out but clearly revitalized when it's time to go, Beau leaping into the back of the station wagon, Arden putting his front paws up on the tailgate so I can do the rest.

We take the Outerbridge Crossing to Staten Island and then the ferry back to Manhattan, leaving the car down in the belly of the boat (no one could know that in nine months' time, this couldn't be done, that the terror that will strike New York will make such a car trip impossible). We go up, the four of us, to the bow of the boat, and though it's cold, we're standing outside, watching the dark gray and tumultuous water over the rail, and the dogs can see it, too, through the square openings in the side of the solid railing, which frame a spume-marked square of rushing water.

I'm looking down at Beau looking into that opening, his nostrils and eyes turned to the water below, and then back up to the horizon line where gray water meets only slightly less gray sky, and it's at this precise moment that something in me breaks.

The purpose of poetry, it has been said, is to bring more of the unsayable into the world of speech, but poetry fails me in my attempt to evoke that moment. It's the weight of every grief I've been carrying. It's the way I've steeled myself to survive Wally's death, over the years of his illness, the death whose sixth anniversary is days away. The way I've willed myself to go on after, bound and determined to be strong enough to continue. It's the way I've fallen in love with Paul, and have loved my hapless, aging dogs, participating in the world of the living while my heart is still shadowed, turned in on its own wound. No matter that it's a minor miracle, in the middle of the great epidemic of my time, that I'm here at all. I am forty-seven; I am on the downward slope of middle age, conscious of the changing of my own body and my own face, mirrored in these aging animals. It's a lifetime of acting strong, saying I won't be submerged—not by my mother's drinking or my father's disengagement, my lousy marriage or the odds against queer people, or the plain daily struggle of being in the world—none of it is going to stop ME, that's what I've always thought, how I've acted. Which is why now, on this blasted ferry, in a bitter early January dusk, the city and its towers just coming into their twinkling details ahead of us, I am about to be knocked over by a wave of vulnerability so large I will not be able to stand up.

Oh I will, on the outside. I will not do what I want to do, which, I am mortified to admit, is to drown myself and my dog. I can see it so clearly: I want to take Beau in my arms, and hold tight to his thinning body, and climb onto the top of the rail, and put my face against his neck, and then I will hold on tight, when we hit that cold water, so that he will not suffer but go down into the cold with me. I have never wanted so clearly to die in my life, I have never felt so little resistance to the impulse.

This is all nearly wordless. I do not articulate what is happening to me, I can't, couldn't begin to if I tried to. My impulse is to close self-protectively around this moment I don't understand and am terrified by. I do not do anything to harm myself, and I swear it's mostly because if I do jump, how will I know that my dear boy will actually drown with me? Won't he want to live, won't he swim as long as he can, and therefore suffer? And, of course, there is the matter of the man beside me, holding onto Arden's leash, who loves me, and would like to have a future, and whom I do not want to harm by making such a brutal, unthinkable rupture. I don't know if he feels it at all, the cataclysm in me that I am hiding because I am so afraid of it. Then and there, my will snaps.

And then the ferry docks, and we make our way back to Thompson Street, park the car in the garage, and, back in the apartment, give each dog the bowl containing his special diet, then find ourselves some dinner in the Village somewhere.

Chapter Eleven

Maybe my will is broken, but I have things to do. On Monday morning, Beau has an appointment with Dr. Cain, so we set out for our familiar walk on East Ninth, but there's something strange in his step. He's okay while we're actually moving, but when we're standing at a curb waiting for the light to change, that wobble in his right hind leg I used to notice in Houston is back, and worse; he doesn't seem quite steady.

The dark shine of that walk persists in memory. Glazed gray morning, chilly and sharp-edged, somehow every single detail picked out by January light. Every blessed element of that neighborhood, the dangerous coil of razor wire gleaming atop scaffolding, sheen of the asphalt where ice had melted, layers of color on a door scrawled with spray paint, erased, tagged again. Odd little scatter of trash in the gutter—all of it evidence, arranged, presented, radiant. As if I were seeing closer to Beau's eyes, wide-open senses, vision charged by the knowledge of limit?

Knowledge of limit. A hesitation in the step, a look in the eyes, something tentative. The opposite of that experience in the park when, kidneys flushed by the vet's irrigating fluids, muscles rebuilding after the shots of Winstrol, he suddenly filled up with the knowledge of his own power.

What does it mean, to say a dog has knowledge of limit? That question is near the core of our living with animals; how much can we know what they feel, to what degree is any description a matter of twisting their animality into a mirror of ourselves?

Once, when I went to give a talk at a distant college, I met a guide dog named Hammer, a golden retriever of notable intelligence. He led the electric cart of his sightless mistress down the rather steep ramp of the aisle to the edge of the stage; there she'd listened to my lecture while Hammer rested on the floor beside her wheels. But when it was time to leave, the aisle wasn't wide enough to allow the cart to turn around, and she would not be able to steer should she try to propel the cart backwards up that long incline.

So, Hammer used his teeth to take hold of a rope attached to the back of the cart, and began to walk, gingerly, backwards, in a very straight line, tugging the cart up toward the entrance of the auditorium. It was the last thing a dog would "naturally" do, walk backwards for forty feet in a very straight line, tugging a weight. What startled me was perhaps not so much that Hammer has been trained to do this unlikely thing, but that he so clearly believed in its absolute importance, the necessity of getting it right. It seemed, this quiet act, a triumph of will and nerve.

Those who don't believe in animal character or intelligence will probably have turned from these pages long ago, and with them safely out of earshot, I can relax into a confident assertion that a dog's eyes may brim with intelligence, preference, temperament, eagerness, forms of memory, assertions of desire. Anyway, if language is metaphor, a system of signs tacked none too firmly to the real, then our words only point imprecisely toward our own feelings anyway, and may as well point just as inexactly toward those of dogs.

A golden retriever is perfectly capable of walking through a city, knowing there will be few such walks to come, and I am certain that his vision might thus be heightened, made more fiercely poignant. And I am likewise sure—through whatever alchemy of bonding takes place between those who live together over years—that his human companion might also be filled with something like dog-vision, his own eyesight taking in something of that shine which death must lend to his animal's sense of the world.

Dr. Cain looks worriedly at Beau's diminished aspect, and then he sees the wobble. "That's not kidney disease," he says. There's something else, something neurological. A brain tumor?

In the past, Dr. Cain has always offered options, even when they were unlikely or extreme. For the kidney problems, he had explained to me, there was a procedure at the Animal Medical Center uptown, a transplant. The cost would be something like thirty thousand dollars a kidney, and even I, who am shamelessly devoted to my dogs, think that's decadent—how could you justify that expense to prolong an animal's life, with all the suffering in the world? Wouldn't it just be more suffering, that surgery—and where *do* those extra organs come from, anyway?

For this new difficulty, though, Dr. Cain presents no choices. He says, "This could move very quickly."

Oh bright shade, friendly ghost, couldn't you come and snatch the black glove of my narrative now?

We're walking home, turning onto Lafayette, when the wobble in Beau's legs gets decidedly worse, he staggers a bit toward a building, and, right beside one of those shuttered metal openings in the street, flung open now for a delivery of rice or beans or who knows what, he falls down. He tries again, and he can't stand up, so he simply stays down on all fours, and looks at me.

I'm kneeling beside him, and I'm trying to hold myself together, and I'm starting to weep. There are passersby who've noticed us; there's a kind woman who says, "Is there something I can do to help?" People in New York, in the majority, love dogs, as if they're grateful for animal presence in the angled and concrete realm in which they dwell. I'm thanking the people who stop, no, he's just having a hard time, I'm saying, but I know his failing is written large on my face, and the woman walks on, with a little exhalation and a look that acknowledges our mutual helplessness. What comes crowding up in me is the wild grief of the ferry, but there's nothing to do but put it away, at eleven in the morning, on a city sidewalk across the street from the Public Theater, and lift Mr. Beau in my arms, carrying him the way, in the Bible pictures of my childhood, shepherds would carry an errant lamb. We head for the apartment, with many stops to rest my arms along the way.

That hour of lead on the Staten Island Ferry—how is it that I looked down at him and knew with absolute clarity that he would die very soon? And how does one arrive at zero and go right on, more or less as if nothing has happened? In truth, I might have done it if it hadn't occurred to me that I would cause him to suffer:

that he was a strong swimmer, that he'd try for a long time to stay afloat, and then his going under would be slow and awful. Or worse, that he wouldn't want to leave me, that he'd keep circling, trying to find me. I couldn't do that to him.

Nor could I do that to Paul, though I'd gone so far down in the tunnel vision of my misery that it was hard to see other people. I was startled, when I showed Paul a story about someone who'd leapt in front of an oncoming train in Hoboken, and his first reaction was, "Oh, that's so cruel to other people, to put them through that!" I truly hadn't even thought of that. The narcissism of depression is a hole with very steep sides.

And, down in the pit, I came up fully, completely, against the absence of hope. What is it that pulls one back? Somehow my faith in human attachments, my belief in the cementing bonds that hold us all together, just wasn't there. It was only the trusting silent fellow at my feet, who kept looking down into the racing wake through the small hole at the base of the ferry railing—it was that trust, that day, that kept me in the world.

Do I dramatize? When I say I want to drown, it's that I am looking for some exit where there is none, some escape from how the world has constellated itself around me. I wouldn't kill myself, but the wish to, the saying of the wish—that's the performance that reveals the truth and points a light toward the seemingly bottomless space opening:

And then a Plank in Reason, broke,
And I dropped down, and down—

On Tuesday, unthinkably, something's wrong with Arden. He's barely touched his breakfast, and now he won't move; he's chosen one spot on the bedroom floor and isn't stirring. We call him for a walk, even go and get the leash and hold it up to him, and he looks at it, with a bleary gaze, and doesn't move. In a while, he moves to another spot on the floor, and drinks some water, but that's it. He's never acted like this in his life.

Is it some kind of sympathetic illness for Beau? Or did something happen at Sandy Hook? Was that wild running in the snowy dunes the thing that pushed both dogs over some edge, brought them to some precipice over which they were already poised to fall?

Wednesday morning, Beau takes his last walk, a lurching stagger with Paul around the courtyard of the Silver Towers, the building next door, where they're a little more dog-friendly, and a rusty Picasso looms in the snowy lawn—a monumental sculpture that seems half woman and half Afghan hound. Arden won't move at all; now we know he's seriously ill. Could it be possible that we are about to lose both our dogs at once?

There's no question of getting Arden to the vet; he's immobile and inert, and Beau, who now can't stand at all, needs attention, too. So, Dr. Cain agrees to come to the house on Friday morning. He arrives with a nurse in tow, the model of brisk efficiency, but, as ever, his MBA demeanor's just the way in which he delivers his compassionate help. There's something strange about our apartment—already a borrowed place, not home but a space that belongs to the university, outfitted rather anonymously for visitors—now become a vet's office.

Beau, who is lying on his spot on the floor where he's taken up residence, sitting like a sculptured greyhound in repose, thumps his tail on the floor when he spies Dr. Cain and the nurse, though of course he can't stand up to greet them. Dr. Cain tries to get Beau on his feet to examine him, but it's impossible; he falls over as quickly as he's propped up. Poor Arden doesn't move at all, head flat on the floor, eyes glazed, when the doctor lifts his lids with a finger. Arden has a high fever. We've almost forgotten that Lyme disease test, and, in truth, he's seemed fine; probably what's happened is that the dormant disease has flared to full-tilt illness.

Dr. Cain talks about how seriously ill both dogs are, and that it would not be inappropriate to euthanize them now.

But there's a chance for Arden—a shot to bring the fever down now, and then antibiotics; it's hard to tell how he'll respond. And Mr. Beau is, after all, watching us all with a look of mild curiosity and pleasure, happy to be in company, and evidently not in pain.

But will he be, later? There won't be any help for us over the weekend. If he's failing and in agony, then what? Dr. Cain will give us a handful of tranquilizers strong enough that six of them crushed up in water will end his life. That's all I need, that emergency measure. Arden gets his medicine, and a measure, if a rather faint one, of hope, and we have recourse, if what's happening to Beau is too much to bear, if we've made the wrong decision in letting him live.

≈≈

We move into a warm circle of lamplight: Beau on the couch, in the spot he used to sneak into when we weren't home but where he now is welcomed. Arden on the rug. Paul and I on the couch, reading, sitting, keeping company, doing nothing. Circle of intimacy. For now, there's no world outside of this room—just a siren or an occasional taxi horn on the periphery, but, in fact, you can barely hear that up here, with the windows closed. I sleep, at night, on the end of the long curve of the sofa—grateful at last for the absurd thing, which seems to have been designed so that a dozen people could watch TV at once. Or, more likely, so there'd be seats for everybody when a class visited the guest professor's digs. I bring Mr. Beau sips of water, raising his head so he can drink. When one of us walks over to him to say hello, and stroke his back and belly, he thumps his tail on the black leatherette. It's so weirdly familiar, uncannily like Wally's illness, the way he's going: the trouble with balance first, and then the legs giving way, and then paralysis, but that unexpected ease and good spirit the whole time, as if it isn't so bad, to go this way, something gentle about it, for the body simply to be shut down gradually from the ground up. Not so gradually, in Beau's case, the paralysis flying up into his torso. We turn him, from time to time, to prevent his lungs from filling with fluid. We stroke him and look into his eyes and talk to him. I'm good at this, putting everything else on hold, to be in this moment with the dying; I'm practiced; there is some deep intimacy about it that feels enclosing, essential.

On Saturday night, Arden staggers up, stumbles in the direction of the balcony, where we've spread out some paper, and pees for a very long time. It's his first movement in three days; it's a wonder. Of course, we always thought our older dog would go first, especially after Tandy Tupper told us about his raggedy heartbeat and his tiny liver—but Arden's a survivor, determined to stay, bless him.

On Sunday morning, I'm sitting on the floor next to Beau's end of the vast couch, drinking coffee. Paul's on the other end, reading a novel by Joy Williams; every time he laughs, Beau thumps his tail. In a while, when Beau's breathing changes, we both kneel beside him. We are talking to Mr. Beau, praising his muzzle and paws and his lovely life, we're holding his face, I'm leaning my head against his belly and praying that he goes easily, trying to send whatever mental force I can muster that might lighten his spirit's way.... Each breath enters his chest a little less deeply. And then, when his breathing's become shallow, he suddenly lifts his head up and back, looking right at me, his eyes widening, with a look not afraid but wondering, startled. A look that would be read, were it a text in a language we knew, as *What's happening to me?* And the life sighs right out of him like a wind, a single breath out and gone.

I go out for a walk, after a time. At the door, I find myself reaching, out of habit, for the leash, and though there's no one to wear it, I put it in my pocket anyway. In a while, I'm standing at the corner in SoHo where, a week ago, Beau caught the scent of soup from a lunch-stand window. His reaction was visceral, physical, eyes going wide with curiosity and delight. Not unlike, I realize, that last look on his face—that what-on-earth look.

Now it's as if I'm down close to the ground, attentive to garbage, splashes of urine on the street, trash in the gutter; I've lowered my head to a dog's-eye view of the city. It's bitter cold. I'm stuffing my gloved hands in my pocket, hanging on to the leash.

I buy a branch of flowering plum, tall apparition in an urban January. Back at the apartment, it goes in a vase beside the end of

the couch where he gave up the ghost, with candles, a photograph
of him years ago, running in the Beech Forest, ears akimbo in the
wind.

⚬⚬

Giving up the ghost—that is the best phrase we have for dying.
The ghost in ourselves, the animating *geist*—in that last moment
of breathing out, I swear it does go *up*.

Transmutation of energy, movement outside of time, release of
the singular into the life of the whole? I don't know what I think
dying is. But when I have seen it, which I have four times now
(three of those deaths are part of this story), I have felt each time
the dying man or animal was, in some essential but unexplainable
way, all right—that is, there was some kindness built into the
structure of things, which, in some fashion, took care of the dead.
That's the best I can do, that rather awkward sentence, to say what
I've seen when I looked directly into that wind.

And you would think such a bit of knowledge would be a tonic
to grief, and I suppose it is, though only very briefly. That moment
of heightened perception only seems to come from being very
close to the dying, from breathing, as it were, with them in the late
hour. That's when the witness might feel the wind blowing from
the other side, as it carries anyone away. But such awareness is not
to be sustained, is not to be carried back into daily life, where
absence and grief reside. I know it's a blessing that he didn't suffer
the long dwindling of kidney disease, that he's been swiftly and
(as far as we can tell) painlessly swept away. But who cares, just
now, about blessings?

⚬⚬

Wherever the rest of him is, Beau's body is right here, in the godawful world of the living, wrapped in an Indian bedspread on the balcony, thirteen stories above the city. In this cold, he's fine there; we can wait a few days and see if Arden—who is beginning to stir again, drinking copious amounts of water—isn't better, maybe well enough to come along to Provincetown, where we'll bury Beau in the garden, in the spot where he used to sit with an eye toward every passerby.

Questions About Time

*H*ere is an ancient problem. *Before the creation of the world, God was alone, but He (I use the pronoun merely for convenience, since there is no adequate one) was also omnipresent. In order to assuage His loneliness by creating a world that was not Himself, there had to be some space in which He did not exist. He did this, the Kabbalists say, by "withdrawing from some region of Himself."*

What is the part of the world that does not have God in it? This place where we find ourselves?

Sometimes I think the place where God is not is time; that is the particular character of the mortal adventure, to be bound in time, and thus to arrive, inevitably, at the desolation of limit. It's why Blake railed at Divinity: If you have form'd a circle to go into, Go into it yourself, and see how you would do.

But then. Perhaps it's in time's hurrying, where everything turns on the wheel toward the crux of disappearance, maybe it's there we could know something of what my friend Lucie calls "an ever," if that quality is to be found or known at all.

Not trying to look outside of time (if such is even possible to us), but farther into it, pushing our faces up toward vanishing, to that

*vaporous line between being here and not. Power that animates and
erases: hello and yes, good-bye and no.*

To look right into the blank behind the eyes of the skull.

To let yourself get used to that wind that blows there.

Chapter Twelve

I t is a marvelous thing, to watch an old dog's obdurate will.

We have very nearly lost Arden, who is eleven years old, but he is the embodiment of resistance and resilience, and now we begin to believe he will see his twelfth birthday. He's walking, tentatively, near the front of our building. He's pleased to ride in the car again, on our trip to Provincetown—though this time Arden sits in the backseat, and naps on a blanket we've spread for him there, because Mr. Beau's curled body lies in the back of the wagon, on our long, sad drive home.

In a little while, we discover how well Manhattan works for the old fellow Arden's become. He can walk out to the sidewalk, plant himself down for a rest, and receive the interest and greetings of passersby; he exerts a particular charm for the elderly, who must find in his infirmity and persistence a familiar mirror. But people of all ages stop to greet Arden. "It's the dogs," Paul says, "who humanize New York." They are occasions of human contact, neighborly conversation, surprising expressions of feeling. We're joined to a community in which we're more likely to be known as Arden's people than by our own names— and, in fact, when we're not with him, we're sometimes not recognized by the very people we speak with when we all have dogs in tow.

Every morning and evening, Arden conducts a social life with the steady stream of dogs that march or amble along the sidewalk. There are a pair of shar-peis he loathes, inexplicably, and, once, a passing Vietnamese potbellied pig fills him with terror—he hides behind us and *shakes*—but otherwise his social congress is harmonious. He carefully gets up, wags a little, sniffs, greets. He receives his human admirers lying on the cement as if he were holding court, expending very little effort.

Though gradually, slowly, he begins to exercise a bit more strength. When we go to the beach at the Jersey Shore, later in the spring, he startles us both by walking down to the edge of the water and, in his old way, flinging himself down on the sand, initiating the movement by dropping one shoulder and then letting the rest of his body follow—and rolling on his back, scratching every inch of spine on the gritty sand and little bits of shell—just the way he has always loved to do.

I'd be grateful if I could mend that way. But I seem to be in two places at once: relieved and glad that Arden's in the world, interested in our new life in the city, and at the same time negotiating with a profound internal sense of emptiness, a blank, a nil spot.

⚜

Despair is, in a way, an appropriate response to the world; how else to face the corrosive power of time, how else to accommodate the brevity and frailty of the self?

Life without an element of despair in it would seem an empty enterprise, a shallow little song-and-dance on the surface of experience. Despair has about it a bracing sense of actuality. Emily Dickinson says, darkly:

> I like a look of Agony,
> Because I know it's true—

Even if it were possible for the psychopharmacologist to engineer our chemical workings away from the experience of despairing, it wouldn't seem wise to do so; what good is a happiness founded on denial? The capacity for despair is probably equivalent to the ability to experience joy; such depths in the self are required in order to make possible the mounting of the heights.

But despair and depression, of course, are not the same thing. Depression is nearly always the *consequence* of despair, a despair one cannot feel one's way through in order to emerge from the other side, a despair that will not be moved. Sometimes such pain—perhaps especially when it has been known for a long time, and all one's resources are used up, depleted—takes hold in the self; it becomes the climate in which we operate, a daily weather. Depression—simply the state of being exhausted by despair?— takes up residence in the desk drawer, the pile of shoes at the bottom of the closet, last night's unwashed dishes tumbled in the sink. Despair is sharp, definite, forceful; it is a response to experience. Depression accumulates, pools, sighs, settles in; it is the absence of a response. It does not make things move. Consider our tropes for it: a cloud, a shadow, a weight. It lingers, broods, sits heavily; it replaces the sharpness of grief (which no one can bear to feel for very long) with the muffling emptiness of fog. Except that I love fog, with its veils and secrets, its lusters and atmospheres. Depression, more precisely, is a kind of dirty haze, and dims everything without adding mystery. It obviates the possibility of surprise. It slows and conceals and stills the circulation of the air.

I'm going to the library, on a spectacularly fine September morning. It's the second day of my new fellowship there, a period of support that will allow me to work on a book, granting me a sustained time to read and think and compose. I'm a little nervous about joining this new community in an unfamiliar setting, which is why I decide I will go ahead and take the train uptown to Forty-second Street, despite the smoking hole in the top of the north tower, that strange, distant shape visible from my intersection on Sixth Avenue. I call Paul on my cell phone. He's home, drinking coffee in our new apartment on Sixteenth Street, getting ready for a faculty meeting at Sarah Lawrence, nervous about his new teaching job—we're both a little wound up about starting something new. I say maybe he'd want to come down to the corner and see.

At the library, everyone's gathered around a computer monitor, watching the BBC news, which has a live camera trained on the towers and is broadcasting the scene over the Web, and that's when the second plane flies into the south tower, and everyone in the room understands that the world we inhabit has changed. On the screen, a pixilated image of the smoking columns of glass and steel. Word of other planes still in the air. Attacks in Washington, in L.A., what else is coming?

And then, one of the twin images on the screen begins, it seems, to consume itself, from the top down, the smoke billowing out only a little before it is sucked down into the great earthward rush and roar. Well, no roar, on the computer screen: a silent, shimmery column of smoke climbs down itself, in a few seconds' time.

Unthinkable thing.

I try to call Paul, but the phone only buzzes; the entire city of New York is trying to make sure somebody's okay, ask what on earth is happening, make a plan, figure out how to get home. The contained city that is the great library at Forty-second and Fifth is pouring out the doors of the building, into the greater pour of people filling the streets. Already the entries to the trains are closed, nothing running.

Even people, bless them, are not running, as if it has been tacitly agreed upon that what is required now is any semblance of order we can make. We will exit Midtown together, get out of here without harming each other. Did someone say get away from the shadow of the Empire State Building? A great mass of humanity is walking down the sidewalks of Sixth Avenue, where I come to understand something I'd never imagined about the end of the world.

Apocalypse is *narrated*, continuously, seemingly endlessly; narration surrounds and encompasses, in layers of sound. People on cell phones—those that still work—are describing what they see, what's in front of them, giving their version of the news. Television sets have been dragged to storefront windows, and the talking heads are delivering their reports while the images of the towers flicker and change. There's a car pulled over by the curb, with its doors open and the radio on loud. People are talking to each other, reciting the versions they know. Someone's talking on a payphone, then stopping to repeat whatever he's hearing to

the people gathered around; the news is coming through head-
sets and boomboxes, repeated and called out. To move down this
sidewalk is to be caught up in a desperate symphonic layering of
talk, reportage, certainty, speculation, questions.

Which ends, at Thirty-fourth Street, as I am in the middle of
the intersection, at a spot where you can see down the avenue the
blunt shape of the north tower, which suddenly seems to descend
itself in that same implosion of smoke. Everyone stops moving.
I have my hand over my heart, involuntarily; some people have
their hands over their mouths; all at once, it's completely quiet.

⋙ ⋘

The Wind didn't come from the Orchard—today—
Further than that—

And if that wind flings a steeple?
There, when I open the apartment door, are Paul and Arden—
did I think they'd be somewhere else? It's a solid, startling relief,
the embrace, and then, of course, we start tumbling out the telling
of what we've seen.

Our place is so new there's hardly anything in it—a round
wooden table, two chairs, a block-patterned needlepoint rug, all
black and gold. Our voices echo. No television yet. We don't
know that this morning, the air over the sidewalks on West Street
was filled with a mist of blood, from those who leapt from the
towers. We don't know how many perished, don't know if the
hospital we hear they've set up on the West Side piers will fill with
the wounded. Don't know, don't know. We decide we should buy
groceries, the first thing people do when a panic begins; much of

New York, those who've made it home, are quickly occupied with stacking canned goods squarely between ourselves and apocalypse. We fill up gallon jugs with water. We listen to the radio. In the afternoon, we go out to Sixth Avenue; our gym's become a rest station for people exhausted from walking. Down the block, there's a corner restaurant that never closes, not even for the end of the world. Everybody there seems plainly grateful for coffee, a sandwich, something vaguely normal. Except for one couple, European kids in stylishly battered clothes, who complain about the restaurant being out of whipped cream. The waiter responds, "Do you know New York was attacked today?"

Back home, we listen to the strange sonic texture of the streets: first, endless sirens, then the traffic slows and stills. So many people walking, walking home, walking downtown to look for someone— by evening, there is no sound at all but the voices and footsteps of people walking by. And then, eventually, not even that. Utter quiet.

The next day, trucks begin to rumble and fly up Eighth Avenue, in the wrong direction, carrying rubble from downtown; they're hauling stuff away as they look for survivors or bodies. The trucks are uncovered; a white ash blows out of them in clouds, a grit that coats the street, our faces and hair. Ash of—what all, exactly? The trucks blare sirens, to warn anyone out of the way, the sound Arden hates most besides gunshots, and I'm grateful he's grown a little hard of hearing, though not enough, it seems, to allay his anxiety.

Anxiety that gets worse, over the coming days, how could it not? When the wind's right, I can smell, myself, the smoke of what the reporters on our new television—we've hurried out to find one, needing, with the rest of the world, to watch the images of our pierced city on the endlessly repetitive news—now call Ground Zero. How long will it burn? Arden can surely smell the nuances and dimensions of what seems to me the scent of burnt plastic. Can he feel not just our nerves but the city's great human unease?

The faces of the missing appear on mailboxes, phone booths, lampposts, walls, shop windows. At Saint Vincent's Hospital on Seventh Avenue, they fill an entire corner, and the crowds stand to read them. In the Union Square subway station, the white-tile walls are a gallery. We start to recognize particular faces. There are identifying details, sometimes oddly intimate things—a birth-mark on a thigh, a hidden tattoo—announced in the texts. The faces themselves are copied, reproduced endlessly, growing further from the original but weirdly more poignant, the more they're duplicated, the longer they're posted.

Every rumble, shadow of a plane. Every shout in the street. Of course, we're shook to the quick. We've taken water and sports drinks, cash, and supplies to the spots where one can donate things; we've gone to Union Square for the vigils that are beginning to be held there, but other than that we feel helpless and immobilized. We are afraid of more attacks, afraid of the response our own nation will make, afraid of the repercussions of the day, the rami-fications.

Ramification is one of those words that we've almost forgotten is a metaphor—it means, literally, branching, consequences of an event branching out from their source. Already we know 9/11 will branch into so many aspects of our lives, into the culture of this country and of the world, in ways we can't even begin to see. We wish that some of those ramifications might involve an understanding of what it has been to live in most of the rest of the world, a clearer sense of how America is seen and what we have wrought. We wish the event itself might be understood in part as a consequence of fundamentalism, a position that chokes off empathy and discourse, stands in the way of community, both abroad and at home. But we're afraid, of course, of where the other branches of that morning will lead.

Sometimes the subway train just stops, and it's dark for a few seconds, and a cold panic seizes my breath till the lights come on. From my desk in my cubicle at the library—I have my own, fluorescently lit, glass-enclosed space, with Venetian blinds to close for privacy—I can feel the distant rumble of the subway beneath Bryant Park, and when that shaking begins, I hold on to my desk every time, my heart racing a little before I remember what it is. A panic that doesn't really fade until the rumbling ends and I'm sure that it was just the subway again.

Despair: how else to accommodate history? Our new millennium began, and it seemed a little bit possible—though surely if we examined the thought too closely, it would evaporate—that a brighter time might be ahead; we have, after all, the round, clean slate of the new number, the row of zeros after the initial digit in 2000. Then the airplanes fly into the great towers, and suddenly it seems that either the twentieth century never ended, with its absurdity of violence, its wild divisions between the privileged and the damned—or else the new isn't a fresh-scrubbed site of possibility after all, but simply an opportunity for a further turning toward brutality, for any sense of civility to further erode.

Arden—like how many citizens of New York City?—has episodes of what seems to be panic. He sits and looks at us, panting, and slaps at the floor with a paw, and won't stop. He wanders, breathing heavily, and sometimes gets in a corner of the apartment, his head against the wall, and just stands there. We wonder if something's happened, back during the days of his high fever, something in his brain? We wonder if it's the smell in the air, the anxiety thrumming in the atmosphere. We try to console him, calm him down. Brushing and soothing helps a little. When we go out, he behaves destructively. There's a set of andirons near the fireplace, which swing if he butts them with his head, and he knocks at them till they fall over. And the heavy folding screen we've put in front of the radiator—one day, he must have butted at that, too, as we come home and find it flat on the floor. Lucky, he's not underneath it.

Then there's anthrax; threats about the mail, fear of mass poisoning. One day, Paul and I go downtown, just because we've heard that the businesses open there are utterly languishing, starving for customers; we're going to do our bit. On the train, we notice that someone has actually sprinkled white powder all over the bench opposite us. People start to sit down, notice it, then walk away.

But, pretty soon, someone else comes along, sets down a shopping bag, starts to move away, then thinks better of it, sighs, sits down. Soon a whole line of travelers and commuters seem collectively to have decided, *The hell with it. We're sitting in the goddamned white powder, spores or no. This is New York City*—and before you know it the whole car is laughing.

※ ※

At the library, I close myself in my cubicle, close the blinds, and turn the big, humming computer on. I read my mail. I write long, detailed e-mails, working for as long as I can. Then I'm done. In a little while, I have my head down on the desk. Outside my door, I hear my colleagues arguing politics, discussing the news. I might go over to my friend Andrea's cubicle, where she is busily not working on her novel. Maybe I'll take a walk, go out for coffee. Maybe lie down on the floor between the desk and the wall, even if it feels a little foolish, to be resting there where I'm supposed to be working, where I'm lucky enough to have the privilege to work. Every now and then, I think about the treasures in the building around me, which seem far away somehow, the books I don't have the energy to read. My mood settles around me, a wool coat that seems to grow heavier with the months in which I accomplish very little—and then, since the coat is too heavy to allow movement, accomplish nothing at all.

Entr'acte

Serotonin

*A*t a writers' conference, I'm speaking on a panel on writers and therapy. At the question-and-answer time—which is, of course, more typically the make-a-statement period—the usual folderol is being tossed about: how writers shouldn't have therapy because it might "interfere with the source of their creativity." "Listen," I want to say, "can you imagine running out of conflicts? Are you serious?" Then someone stands up and says the alarming and predictable thing: "Well, if van Gogh had medication, we wouldn't have all those masterpieces, would we?"

I can't help but reply, "I think we'd have a lot more of them."

Which, I guess, is a way of saying that a little serotonin reuptake inhibitor seems to have saved my life. It became clear, in those dire days of dragging myself to the library, that I couldn't get out of the slump by myself. And truly I don't care if this is the placebo effect at work or not, the moment when suddenly I feel a change: I'm standing at an intersection on Eighth Avenue, waiting for the WALK sign, and I feel a shiver up my spine, and the sudden impulse to hold my head up, to stand up straight—how long has it been? And something within me looks around at the world and says, "Oh, right, here I am."

Do I look a little like the lost Arden, called back to himself when those benevolent strangers called his name?

Here, *on a low dose of Celexa, turns out not to be a muffled place at all—rather I am able to feel highs and lows instead of that self-protective interior cloudiness that keeps everything dim, turned down, because the low is just too dangerous to admit. The drug is neither a numbing dose of bliss nor escape from conflict, by any means. Those who've needed and benefited from SSRIs understand that they do something else, which is to provide a kind of platform, figuratively, on which the psyche can stand; they keep you from sinking to an untenable depth. If Dickinson felt when "a Plank in Reason, broke"—then serotonin seems to be what puts that plank back in place underneath us, that bit of safety. Which isn't to say you aren't then sad, or over-whelmed by the world—only that you are capable of feeling some-thing besides numb. The right dose means I'm out of the joyless pit, that I can go back to feeling what Freud called "ordinary misery."*

All my life, I've possessed a certain buoyancy, an ability, in difficulty, not to be held under, to rise back up—my head above the waters, like Mr. Beau swimming the Great Salt Lake. But now that seems to have deserted me. Age? Exhaustion? Something as apparently simple as the death of a golden dog? It seems a miracle to find some version of that spirit of lightness in a small, pink, ovoid tablet.

To that, to that marvel, all praise and gratitude.

And if, in fact, we didn't have so many van Goghs? The painter himself, given the choice, might well have preferred to live.

Chapter Thirteen

West Forty-sixth Street is the outer edge of the theater district, slightly on the skids, permanently referring to a brighter past. But energetic, nonetheless: these old brownstones have been hollowed and tunneled into piano bars and cabaret rooms, and in their intricate warrens persists the stuff of another moment. We thread our way through the fizz and bustle on the street, taxis arriving, steam funneling up out of a hole in the pavement, dissipating in shreds in the air like bursts of stage fog. Barkers hawk their shows, and glossy photographs of singers are glassed in little boxes, surrounded by strings of lights. No one seems to pay any attention to any of them.

Paul and I have come to see an old-fashioned drag performance, a man who becomes Judy Garland, late on Saturday nights, in a basement cabaret. Through the padded black vinyl doors, we enter a narrow, extremely loud piano bar, packed with people practically shouting the lyrics to some old party tune. They seem to be working alarmingly hard to have fun, and it's a relief to wind our way out of their jostle to the dim hall at the back that leads to the cabaret room. We're asked by a slight, fey man behind the red velvet rope, who might be the ancient keeper of a temple, if we have a reservation, but our lack of one doesn't seem to be a problem. We're led to a table right near the front, and seated inches from two women in similar black pantsuits and elaborate blond coiffures. Somehow, they remind me of a pair of chandeliers; it must be the sculptural upsweep of the hair combined with their high degree of collective sparkle: rings, pins, sequins, necklaces. The friends are ablaze, their eyes lit by cocktails. I notice the one beside me is wearing black silk pants embroidered with dozens of tiny martini glasses.

They also very much want to have fun. While we're chatting, I keep taking little pauses to glance around the room, the unlikeliest assembly of an audience I have ever seen. Behind Paul sits a large woman with unruly black tresses and huge, black, horn-rimmed glasses bound at the corners by tape; she appears to be wearing her bathrobe. Here is an assortment of old queens, wearing clothes they might have saved since the last time they saw the *real* Judy: slender cardigans, skinny ties, plaid sport coats from another age. A knot of drunken Japanese businessmen, talking furiously, toasting, aglow; three geriatric women, each in a loose beaded top, heads nodding ceaselessly, as if they sat in silence, perpetually saying no to something they could not abide. A young straight couple who seem to have been given someone else's unwanted tickets.

All the lights in the room fade to black, and suddenly the little stage blazes: a man in black races up the aisle to the piano and begins a florid overture threaded with phrases from "Over the Rainbow." Then, beneath big white letters proclaiming JUDY over a curtain of black velvet, appears our star. He's an energetic little butterball: Judy overweight, on the edge of decline, but still in good concert voice. He's a forthright belter of a singer, acutely tuned to Garland's vocal mannerisms, and he launches right into one of the signature songs, stepping back and forth in that funny little movie-musical dance step that Garland just couldn't seem to stop doing. He's wearing a black skirt and jacket over a glittery top (just like the ones those three nodding Fates in his audience have on tonight), a short black wig, and, though his pitch wobbles a bit, I have to admit he's incandescent, especially on the ballads, just the right note of breathy sorrow, a vulnerability breaking open beneath the will to go on.

First, I forget that he doesn't look a thing like Judy. Then, as he keeps singing, I forget he's a man, then I pretty much forget he's not Judy. Well, he *is* Judy, isn't he? In that he's an embodiment of her image, the continual broadcast streaming out from her vanished, original self, a potent cocktail of stamina and damage, heart and amphetamine. Once, there was one Judy, the broken survivor, then there were thousands, her ghost itself fragmented into a legion of apparitions. Drag has moved far beyond those days; a fierce new crop of drag queens impersonate no one but themselves. But even they seem now a little historical; drag's moment of cultural visibility has passed. In this late hour, it seems there's only one Judy again, or at best a few, the rear guard of the drag world, and this one's singing her heart out to an odd assortment of believers in Midtown on a late Saturday night.

In James Merrill's epic vision of the afterlife, the souls of those to whom the living repeatedly turn for instruction or inspiration—Rilke, Jesus, Mohammed—are pale wraiths; they've been mined again and again until their essential, illuminating ore is all but exhausted. But here I think JM got it wrong; even the weariest of archetypes is capable of renewal by the force of experience. New circumstances shock them awake; the turn of events refreshes even the most tired of wellsprings. Surely, you'd think Judy Garland—a gay cliché, grown musty as even the notion of "gay" becomes encrusted, itself a cliché—you'd think Miss Garland, as our friend Murray, a seventy-year-old gay man who used to book her tours, always refers to her—Miss Garland should simply be fading away like a faint old radio signal, shouldn't she?

But she is alive and well, this evening, and what has brought her hurtling back from the void is the rip in the body of the city, the still-raw wound of "the events of September 11." (That phrase has become the standard tag for the chaos that broke upon New York, just as the rumbling war machine generates new, interchangeable catch phrases: Infinite Justice, Enduring Freedom.)

Judy has not been blind to these days. She has a purpose; she wants us to know that the only tolerable response to suffering is persistence. While her demeanor and her voice announce the presence of pain, the songs she chooses refuse to dwell in grief. She ransacks the storehouses of consolation, though in truth her advice all seems to be the same: summon the grit to persist. *Smile, though your heart is breaking,* she sings, and *Lose that long face.*

Then she's actually singing that song from *Carousel*—*When you walk through a storm / hold your head up high / and don't be afraid of the dark*—a song through whose grander passages our voices used to career till they wrecked hopelessly on the high notes, back in seventh-grade chorus. She really isn't bad, though her triumphant moment is Stephen Sondheim's "I'm Here," a song written after

Judy's death, so that her thrilling final assertion—*I've been there, and I'm here*—seems to ring on many levels at once. Judy is dead and still singing. She has survived the zero, annihilation, and it hasn't stopped her; therefore, we who took heart once from her supernatural strength, might we not do as she enjoins? The chandelier-women nod; they look to us for acknowledgment; it's true, isn't it, we have to pick ourselves up, dust ourselves off. The waiter arrives with the compulsory second round of drinks.

Judy sings a song from *Valley of the Dolls*, "I'll Plant My Own Tree," which sends the young straight woman into ecstasy; it is just the moment she's wanted, and she cries out in delight. Then Judy's eye is caught by the young woman's boyfriend. She steps down from the stage to look him over; she wiggles a little with delight. "Oh," she says, "I have dresses older than you!" Pause. Three beats. "But that's all right. As long as we're all here together"—pause, exhalation of air, pause again—"it's a party!"

And on she goes, into the introduction to "San Francisco":

I never will forget Jeanette MacDonald,
to think of her it gives me quite a pang.
I never will forget the way that old Jeanette
stood there in the ruins and sang . . .

Judy, of course, doesn't stand in the ruins; she *is* the ruin. In this way she enthralled a generation of gay men, singing her way out of suffering while still bearing the inescapable marks of damage. That was her undeniable, energizing paradox: she could stand before her audience in both transcendence and degradation at once. It was a stance that gay men instinctively understood.

And now the paradox is taken one step further: Judy's dead and still singing, her flickering image recedes into the distance but she's still pouring her heart out, in this dark little room on the western edge of Midtown. And, of course, she isn't real, merely a phantom, and thus she can say, beneath the words she's singing, these terrible things: youth fades, beauty passes, what is tender turns dark or dissolves, pleasure fades, the drumbeat suffering of the world drums on, and what is there to trust but that things end?

But that's all right, as long as we're here . . .

There is a point where any adult attempt at understanding becomes an absurdity. Eventually, we look at the griefs we're offered by experience, and there we are: inconsolable, powerless to dispel their weight through rationalization or acceptance. That is what seems to unite every disparate soul in this room, finally: we're all helpless.

⁂

Once, a young poet said to me, "It's really too easy to take loss as your subject, isn't it?"

I wanted to say, "Yes, dear, and I've had so much choice in the matter." Though I said nothing of the kind.

In fact, writing about grief has never been any kind of a choice; when I've resisted it, the need to articulate has simply insisted all the louder. I have never been able to accept the fact of limit. Though I have had nearly fifty years to think about it—I have now lived longer than Judy did, in her corporeal form!—I am no more reconciled to it than ever. I'm a ruin, too, and I stand here on my small, dark stage with these phrases tumbling out of my mouth. Judy, of course, isn't reconciled, either, but she has a form into which she pours her grief and exaltation, and so do I.

—·—

In truth, most of us in this room just now seem to have had quite enough of looking loss square in the face, thank you. The women at the next table, who seem to have become our dates, grin, agree, and blaze. Judy says, *Pack up your troubles in your old kit bag.* Her audience seems to accept this instruction when it comes from her, because she herself cannot quite do it, because she is so obviously a wreck through and through. That's how she gains her credibility. The towers, both public and private, tumble, and she can't pack up her troubles any more than we can. But she is still here, isn't she, singing on the cabaret stages of the afterlife?

I think of old Mr. Arden, trundling his way up the stairs.

A Show

*A*rden used to like to climb on a bed and roll on his back, and, for our pleasure and his own, growl and speak and emit whatever range of sounds he could muster. This always delighted us, and we'd rub his belly, or one of us would take hold of his front legs and the other the rear, and we'd say, "Stretch him out, stretch him out!" and pull a little on him to lengthen his spine while he growled and talked some more. We used to call this "putting on a show," and it seemed to fill Arden with happiness. As if now he could do what we always did, and show us he also could fill the air with sounds.

Chapter Fourteen

An early reservation for Thanksgiving dinner is the only one we can get, at the old house near the harbor converted to a fancy restaurant, but it turns out to be just right. At two o'clock, the staff is fresh, the turkey and its roasted and glazed accompaniments perfect, and the desserts so complicated as to silence our conversation and demand full participation. I have cinnamon ice cream with a pear poached in zinfandel and floating on dark chocolate. Time for a walk.

Arden's walking well again, not the heedless hurry of the old days but not the awful hobbling of the spring and summer, either. Now he manages a slow stroll along the Beech Forest paths, even a little burst of running at the sight of a bird, or at a turn into a new part of the woods. I am thinking of Beau's big paws on these same paths all those years; that sound's still with me, the solid thud of four big paws, the lovely little thunder of him racing ahead. That never exactly leaves. Somehow, *memory* seems too slight a word, too evanescent; this is almost a physical sensation, the sound of those paws, and it comes allied to the color and heat of him, the smell of warm fur, the kinetic life of a being hardly ever still: what lives in me.

And just as I'm feeling intensely grateful for that—well, a gratitude commingled with sadness, which certainly is an admixture I can live with, which might, in fact, be a sort of concrete upon which an adult life is built—just as I am thinking of that, on the autumn path, scents and tones of leather, brass, resin, brandy, tobacco, leaf mold, mushrooms, wet bark—I think, *Paradise*. Then I think, *If there's a heaven and he's not there, I'm not going*.

And then the corrective voice: *The kingdom of heaven is within you*.

Just the other night, at dinner in a restaurant on Eighth Avenue, our friend Marie said, "The kingdom of heaven is within you. Think about that," she said. "Within YOU." We'd been talking about September 11, wanting to go to church, and how inadequate any religious institution we could find felt. Marie and Paul both grew up Catholic, and have an inbuilt longing for a community of the spirit, a pattern of ritual. Marie started telling us about a group called The People of the Way, a little gathering of students of early Christianity, who attempt to practice something like the rigorous and humane discipline of the early church. "If you asked THEM if Jesus was God," she said, "they'd have gone *hah!*" (Here she made a dismissive face and a big gesture.) "They believed what Jesus said: the Kingdom of Heaven is within you. Auden said as soon as Christians stopped believing that, that was it—then we got the Church, hierarchy, mediation, corruption. But before that. Within you."

We tried to imagine what would happen if people really believed that.

A little research on the original New Testament Greek raises more questions than it answers. The first problem is that preposition: you can read it as meaning "within," "among," "amid," or "near at hand." Then things get more complicated by that last pronoun, which turns out to be a plural version of "you." English-speakers are always seeking ways to make up for the absence of a second-person plural—*y'all, youse, yez, you guys*—depending on which part of the country you're from. Any of which sounds truly dreadful when appended to *The Kingdom of Heaven is within*...

And, therefore, you could read the statement as meaning that the heavenly realm resides in the individual spirit, or that it arises in the context of communal exchange. Or, I suppose, both, if you can manage to negotiate both private and collective heavens.

Night conversation on the train. At night there's no world out there, or hardly any—just the dark of the window, made darker by the bright overhead lights inside the train. The world narrows down to the overheard conversations of the passengers around me on their cell phones, and the book I'm reading, and then the drifting off that comes after a long day and the rhythmic motion of the train car. I'm slipping back into darkness, then Mr. Beau says, *You've got to let me go.*

No, not Mr. Beau, who does not, after all, speak, even in death.

Something else—puppet dog in my internal theater, character in a night-train play?

He says, *Your grief keeps me tied to you.*

I say, *I'm doing that?*

He says, *I want to run with the other dogs, and swim with the seals!*

I say, *But how would I let you go?*

He says, *Cry over me until you're through.*

I say, *But then you'll be gone?*

No, he says, *but I'll be different.*

Long pause.

I'll be there, he says, *anywhere in the world you are. But you've got years to go.*

I say, *Then I'll see you again?* But then already I'm not letting him go, am I?

Let's say heaven is only available through the individual imagination. No external route, no way for anyone to bring you there. Grace might descend, in its odd, circuitous routes: we are visited by joy, seem to be given a poem or a song, something we encounter fills us to the rim of the self. Those things point the way, but who lives in that heightened awareness? And if we could, would despair be defeated? Balanced, at least? Of course, there must be sorrow in heaven, but can paradise contain the hopelessness of despair, is heaven that much of a paradox?

My country forebears thought of heaven as a place devoid of tension, without conflict. But they lived hardscrabble, hand-to-mouth lives, after all; my mother's father scraped together fifty cents a week, for decades, so that when he died he could have a decent funeral. His wife cut up her one good dress to make a shroud for a daughter. There was never enough. No wonder they'd figure heaven as a place of plenty, all needs met, eternal completion and praise.

But I can't imagine anything that far removed from the rest of the universe; isn't every place permeated by tension, the play of opposites, the yoked, irresolvable contradictions? And if the kingdom of heaven is within us, then that means that what is within us must fit into the kingdom of heaven, doesn't it?

Despair, then, isn't a place we leave—some kind of psychic location we pull into, look around, then pull out of again, relieved not to have to live there. It's more like a dimension of the self, which, once opened, is part of us forever; a pole within, a spot of darkness, deeply magnetic (God abandoning a dimension of Himself?). Without it, might we just float away, unable to feel the darkness and suffering of the world? The adult self requires balance; if we don't internalize some of the terrible gravity around us, we might as well not have been here at all. One sees people like that, untouched, perpetually young faces who seem merely to have floated through life (forgive me, spirit of empathy, for my rush to judgment, but certain airbrushed Chelsea boys come to mind). They are inevitably beautiful at first glance, and less so on developing acquaintance, not enough of life has entered them to transform and solidify their characters.

I'll take a ruin over a brand-spanking-new tract home any day; real beauty is always marked by the passage of time; it dwells in time; its loveliness increases as the workings of age and the mysteries of continuing enhance it; even Grecian urns, those brides of quietness, are more beautiful because of their small cracks, the mellowing of their paint, the fine and subtle darkening of the stone.

I think we have to let a part of us be abandoned by God.

But gaining any measure of control over the degree of darkness in the self is a damnably hard thing; too much and we're weighed down, missing a sense of the world's brightness; a bit more and we're unable not just to see but to act, immobilized by that muffling, heavy overcoat, worn winter and spring alike, which will not allow us to breathe, will not allow us to see and be seen.

So what pulls us back, what keeps the balance?

At the Cézanne show: consummate, weighted fruits, their physical heft *made* out of green, or red, coexist with skulls, smoking candles. Not one or the other. The skull's just as solidly, deftly *there* as every other element of the scene, the bone given the same exacting attention as any apple or pear—attention rendered in the paint, in exact strokes, placed, just so, in a quick gesture won with the eye's long attention.

When my grandfather died—he of the carefully kept up insurance payments, to foot the bill for a good-sized funeral—I was two. My sister, who's ten years older, tells me what I don't myself remember: how there was a big Irish wake in the house, and everyone brought something, and sat and ate and drank around the open casket late into the night. Our cousin Buddy, who was in the military, brought a huge box of doughnuts, and Sally and I spent the whole night drinking coffee spiked with whiskey, and helping ourselves to one doughnut after another. Coffee, whiskey, sugar, an open coffin—perfect beginnings for an elegiac poet, no?

Paul and I have gone to see my favorite opera, *The Magic Flute*, a fairy tale, a children's pageant that can say the most serious of things because it claims no stake in the real; we are not expected to believe. In this production, there's a particularly compelling staging of the scene where, as part of their initiation into the mysteries, Tamino and Pamina must pass through the dangerous elements: fire and water. What will protect them?

Pamina rests her hand on her lover's arm, and Tamino lifts his little flute and begins to play, while around them rise the tongues of flame, element that burns and cleanses. Together, they walk through the flames—played by dancers under glowing light, they look surprisingly convincing, flickering and forking out—unharmed.

And then, again, she rests her hand on his proffered sleeve, he lifts his instrument, and plays his whistling tune—such a delicate, almost childlike little song, to carry us through such struggle!—and together they pass through the waves, those same dancers now lit blue, performing as the unbreathable element that both drowns and washes clean.

It makes me take Paul's hand, in the dark. Isn't it strange how the piping little air—in the midst of the great constructions of sound Mozart pours out so effortlessly—how that tune's the bravest, finest thing?

Thus, in the face of all dangers, in what may seem a godless region, we move forward through the agencies of love and art.

⸙⸙

What if the kingdom of heaven is the realm of paradox? Attachment and detachment, they flip back and forth like lenses the optometrist shows you: this one, or this one, which is better, which is more clear? You are abandoned by the world and at once wholly loved by it. You are the little baby in arms of time, and time will carry you away. You're given memory, buoyancy, humor, humility, and friendship, as well as forgetfulness, heaviness, lament, self-pity, and isolation. You're the crown of creation, and fodder for every little mite and laboring insect that carries the earth's own children back into the dirt. Everything and nothing. This is it, what surrounds you, the daily life to which you are much of the time asleep—this is it, and this was it the whole time.

Drugs for Arden

E levil: *for those bouts of anxiety after September 11, prescribed by a doctor straight out of Central Casting for a Chelsea vet: designer muscle, sleek, blond hair, and a soul generally untouched by struggle, or perhaps mortally afraid of it; I probably diminish him, but that's how he comes across. The pill seems to work; Arden's calmer for a couple of weeks, and then has a perfectly awful, intractable anxiety attack, at which point I throw the Elevil away, and Arden promptly seems much better.*

The same doctor prescribes raw foods, *a diet prepared by an industrious soul here in the neighborhood and sold in the doctor's office frozen, in plastic tubes like sausage, a mixture of beef and barley, lamb and oats, chicken and wheat. The idea is to replicate the diet of dogs in the wild, back someplace before domestication, on the theory that their bellies have not further evolved since then, and that the enzymes and particular merits of the food are destroyed by the cooking and canning that create the usual product.*

It seems mostly reasonable, except for maybe the evolutionary part, and Arden thinks it all right, or tolerable anyway, and a small fortune is thus consigned to bags of the stuff, a daily regime of which certainly costs more than the contribution one is asked to make per day to feed a child through one of those charities that promise to nourish the hungry in Africa or Latin America. It is only a matter of weeks, though, before Arden refuses to have any more to do with raw foods, walking disdainfully away from the bowl.

Rejection of Chinese herbs, recommended by the acupuncturist who makes house calls, is much more swift. I'm an expert in making pills into palatable little packages, rolled in bits of ham, disguised in balls of cheese or peanut butter, hidden in balls of dog food like Swedish meatballs—though, in truth, even when I think I've succeeded in slipping something by, it's not all that unusual to find, hours or days later, some discarded pill discreetly stashed in a corner someplace. But there is no hesitation about the green, fragrant Chinese herbs; they're immediately, unequivocally spit out, and no amount of persuasion or coercion avails.

Acupuncture, a recommended cure for those troubled hips, and a treatment from which I myself have benefited, is better tolerated. Arden sits patiently with the needles in place, though every now and then he insists on moving, and the little stainless steel needles tumble onto the carpet. Is he better? Hard to tell. But he clearly dislikes the acupuncturist a bit more with each visit, until that throaty growl begins to make me nervous, and I figure I'd best listen to the patient's wishes.

Chapter Fifteen

After our long, scorching taxi ride over the hills, it would make sense to take a nap—but once we've opened the double wooden doors that lead out onto the terrace of our room, it's impossible to even think of it. We look out over rooftops and gardens; San Miguel de Allende, a hill town in the high desert north of Mexico City, is stacked, terraced, red-tiled, painted every shade of rose, brick, and ocher, with jolts of electric blue thrown in. Down the hill's long decline, a valley opens out, tiny distant trees and spires and lake in a smoky expanse, like the background in some Renaissance painting. The world smells like burning mesquite, diesel fuel, very old wood, sage, geraniums, and dust. In the street below us, buses and cars thread their way between groups of people, children and dogs and adults strolling, vendors with dolls, a man with a tall stack of straw hats on his head, a table laid out with *helados* and *frutas* and golden, round *empanadas*. We'll sleep later.

Once out the heavy, carved doors of the hotel (every place seems to have these, tall, armored with ancient hinges and locks), we discover that the narrow roadway has filled with a parade. It's Three Kings Day, the Mexican feast of the Epiphany. A succession of trucks grind their way up the street; on the flatbed of each, a glorious display of children and animals, all costumed to represent moments in the early life of Christ.

Though, in fact, it's the Virgin Mary who's the center of attention. Here she is, with Joseph, bent over the rough cradle, receiving the attentions of the kings; now she and Joseph are fleeing into the desert, perched on an amazingly cooperative donkey. Now they are camped at an oasis, surrounded by boy angels and baby goats. In each scene, the Virgin's portrayed by a girl wrapped in blue, attending to her role with gravity. The angels look around, and even wave back at us when we wave to them, and one of the Josephs wobbles noticeably as the truck lurches a little on a pothole. But each Mary is radiantly fixed, her attention focused on the doll in the manger or in her arms.

San Miguel's a complex place. A thriving expatriate community, Americans and Europeans who've settled here, along with wealthy weekenders from Mexico City, have brought coffee bars, Internet cafés, ATMs, a very good restaurant that inscribes its name on every slice of its delicious chocolate cake. There's a venerable art school, and an unfinished Siqueiros mural in an old convent turned Centro de Bellas Artes. Various residents are involved, this week, in a festival honoring the work of Virginia Woolf.

In the next parade, the three kings ride through town on horseback, tossing pineapple candy to everybody along the street, followed by a delirious cast of celebrating characters: Bugs Bunny and the Devil, Barney the Dinosaur, Uncle Sam and Minnie Mouse. Bells from I don't know how many churches mark seemingly random hours of the day. People wander into mass and prayers and first communions, into the temples of the images: Virgins whose faces are lit by tenderness, or transfixed by grief, boy saints who seem the incarnation of devotion, fiercely suffering Christs revealing their blazing wounds. The two thieves writhe in the air on crosses of their own. Each church is a box full of such carved and costumed emblems of the possibilities of human feeling. People wander out again to circle the *jardin*, or laugh at clowns, or sit in the benches under the clipped laurels. The garden's so densely planted and ordered that it seems larger than it actually is, a dreamy public space made for both social life and private reflection, for festival and for respite. Ancient women, cowboys, the ubiquitous beloved children, the man who sells newspapers meticulously folding his stock.

Exactly the opposite of an American suburb, where few people are visible, everyone held apart in their privacy. There commingling happens by driving—either because we're all on the road together in our separate vehicles or because we've driven someplace, mall or restaurant or church, where we can actually *see* each other. Here, people seem to be in the streets a great deal of the time, seeing their friends and acquaintances and everyone else as well, selling things and shopping, hanging out, consuming, enjoying, taking pleasure.

Paul and I are entranced by this fabric of urbanity so unlike our own. In New York, of course, there's a continuous, vital presence of people on the streets, but nothing like this sense of coherence and connectedness. Our city's essential characteristic, in fact, is difference, disparate humanity thrown together in the simultaneous adventure and near-disaster of the everyday. But once much of the world must have been like San Miguel, a place where so much is known and held in common; it feels like walking into a tapestry, that tightly woven, and every corner quick with life.

I'm walking down a steep side street when a woman comes up the opposite direction, leading three beautiful burros loaded with firewood. The animals are short, wide-bellied, on their backs are woven serapes, and on top of those, canvas sacks filled with neatly stacked sticks, a cargo of firewood. It's like a movie of Mexico, such a perfect image out of another age. And then I look a little farther down the street, and see on the corner the boom, the dolly that hoists a beetling black camera. It *is* a movie.

But the next day, we're walking near the Parque Juarez, a tropical garden where dogs lope through the heat to drink from stone fountains placed at each intersection of the diverging paths, and along comes a fellow with three less photogenic burros—a little scrawnier and a bit less doe-eyed—and there's not a camera in sight. The town's specifically itself and an image for consumption, both a replica and an original at once.

The next day, there's a dog. We've been noticing the dogs of San Miguel all along, not just the solitary drinkers in the park but the ones who wander the streets at all hours, day and night, often with a purposeful attitude, an evident sense of destination. Some wear collars, some do not; some look well fed, others obviously lean. They dart in and out of traffic with abandon; we think it's a wonder they're still on earth. Most seem quite pleasant in their demeanor, if not overly concerned with us; they accept a pat or a friendly greeting, and then either head on their way or remain placidly in place, enjoying the warmth of sunlight in a doorway, or waiting attentively on someone who's soon to return.

But the dog we meet late on Calle Canal is different. We're headed back to the hotel when she comes creeping out from behind a parked car, checking us out. I call to her, and she starts, a little suspicious; she's learned to be careful around people. I squat down with my hand out in front of me, and though she's evidently scared, she's also eager, so she comes over, wags her tail tentatively, holding her head tensely so she can rapidly pull away from a kick or a blow aimed in her direction.

And then I discover that she is delightful.

She sits carefully in front of me, looks up expectantly. I reach out my hand for her to sniff—she draws back a little, then decides it's safe, and inspects my knuckles. I scratch the top of her head, between her ears, and she cocks her head and narrows her eyes in evident delight. I bend down closer, taking her in: she's short-haired, yellow, a mix of who knows what, definitely influenced by retrieverish genes, though she's smaller than any Lab, and her little ears suggest that ubiquitous, skinny no-breed that street dogs in Mexico seem to evolve or devolve toward, away from the specificity of pure breeds. She's thin but not emaciated, and young as she is—no gray hairs on that face, a smoothness that suggests youth—she must have already borne a litter of puppies, since her nipples are enlarged and purplish. Where on earth are they now, those babies? She places her delicate head in my two hands, giving me the weight of it, which seems almost nothing at all, the weight, maybe, of an orange. There's an odd moment of connection between us, which I experience as an intensity, a moment lit by a sort of surprise—is it arrogance to think no one has ever shown her this sort of affection before? It's as if she's drinking it in, and at the same time assessing me as a potential companion, a source of rescue or dinner. She is weighing me, as I weigh her small head, and we are finding each other good.

We walk down the street to the small market to buy her something to eat; she trots along behind, interested. The market's closed. We turn back toward the hotel; she follows, meanders into traffic, comes back to us. Now we don't know what to do; we don't want to encourage her, because we're going in to bed, and how can we help her? She walks away from us, back into the street, squats to pee, oblivious to the oncoming bus. She pees and pees; the bus comes to a stop, waits, then the driver loses patience and starts to inch forward, and still she doesn't move, until one of us runs over and calls her out of the street.

Now we're back at the hotel steps. Obviously, she can't come in; there's a bellman lurking around the *entrada*, and he seems to be viewing these proceedings dimly. She isn't about to leave. Paul's had enough; he thinks there is nothing in the world we can do for her, and he's tired and wants to go to bed. Not only can I not just walk away, I don't think she'll go if I do. I sit down on the steps with her; she lies down beside my feet. What do I think I'm doing? Paul goes in, the hovering bellman glowers, I sit on the tiled steps with this suddenly devoted creature. My mind starts racing: is it possible that I could bring her into the hotel room? And then?

A group of women hotel guests appear; they greet me—"Oh, look what you've found!"—and the dog gets up to inspect them. They're busy petting her, she's engaged in sniffing, checking out their bags, hoping they've got something edible stowed away, and that's my opportunity to slip away and head up the labyrinth of stairs—part sheltered, part open to the stars—that leads to our rooftop room.

As soon as I'm there, I get out to the terrace; I see the bellman shooing the dog away. She crosses the street, sits down, looks back. She trots back to the hotel steps (more hazardous traffic, nearly stopping my heart), and the man shoos her again. Back across the street. She's looking for me. I go in.

My mind's racing; Paul and I start talking about our options. We're leaving in a day; we don't know the first thing about importing a dog. I've heard stories of long quarantines, stringent health regulations. I have visions of myself trying to get on a plane from Leon to Houston, and then another from Houston back to Newark, attempting to explain to customs officials of two countries about this mutt I've picked up on the street. When we entered Mexico, there was a separate tent for people bearing agricultural products; they didn't even *mention* animals. Everyone getting off the plane had to walk through an outdoor pavilion in which we were sprayed with a suspicious mist that smelled of some debased, chemical version of orange blossom—what *was* that stuff? A universal pesticide? We joked, at the time, about how much of our immune systems might remain after *that*. If we had to be doused in a toxic mist, what would they do with a street dog?

It seems impossible. I go back out to the balcony, don't see her anywhere, and then I do: she's found a stoop, elevated six feet above the sidewalk, a hundred feet from the hotel door. She's curled up there, on the concrete, her goldish body visible in the moonlight. She's made herself round and small. I go back in, my mind still hurrying, flooded with some combination of tenderness and guilt. I say to Paul, feeling my voice choke as I do so, "It's so unfair. Why should I have everything and she have absolutely nothing at all?"

Paul says he has to believe that something may happen for her, that someone will take her in, that like the many dogs on the street here, she'll find a way to manage on her own.

Maybe he's right, but there's her seeming indifference to the particularly scary fact of Mexican traffic, in which the life of one more dog may not count for much. And she's suddenly a crystallization, for me, of something on the periphery of my vision all week here—how we think nothing of dining in restaurants where our dinner might cost more than some of the people we pass on the way there will see in a month. How easy it is for us to enter the ancient churches and take esthetic delight in those wounded, grieving Cristos, with their alarmingly penetrating glass eyes—which for the faithful are mirrors of their own Calvaries. My pleasure in these sculptures is not purely formal; I love the way they seem to embody the pain of the world, enacting the suffering of God as a mirror and crux of human grief. But still I understand they cannot mean for me in the same direct, unambiguous way they do for their intended audience. I'm cushioned by the accident of birth; I'm *norteamericano*, white, a college professor who makes his living as a poet, for heaven's sake, a teacher of poetry. I have a plane ticket home, an old house by the sea, an apartment in the city. And the dog asleep on the concrete stoop beneath my balcony cannot expect even a bowl of water in the morning.

After my restless night, she's gone. I begin asking some questions. It turns out it's not as hard as I thought, according to our new American friends who live here half the year: a clean bill of health from a Mexican vet is the basic ticket out. Is it actually possible that we could, in twenty-four hours, get her to a willing doctor, certify her, get an appropriate crate, arrange for her to travel on two airplanes, and arrive with her in New York on Saturday night? Perhaps. But we don't do it. For one thing, there's Arden, at home with our friends Patrick and Cordelia, who've moved in for the week to take care of him. In truth, our trip has been darkened only by worrying about him. We haven't left him with anyone since his illness, and reports from Cordelia haven't been good—he's sleeping badly, panting with anxiety, and when she must leave him alone, he usually knocks something over, trying to break something in the house. We know he's happiest when Paul and I are in bed together, with him in between us, one of us resting a hand on his flanks; then he knows where we both are; then there is no need to search, no occasion for confusion. How could we expect him to deal with a new dog?

Soulful though she might be, she's a girl of the streets, too; a new acquaintance here says the street dog he adopted bit him twice. We have no idea who she'd turn out to be. Well, that's not quite true; I trust that moment, the weight of her small head in both my hands; who she is, in that instant, became perfectly clear. You can know an animal—or a person, for that matter—in an instant, really, though your understanding can go on unfolding for years. And she'd be fine in New York; here in San Miguel, too many people and cars are held in a space designed for the seventeenth century, and the result is a density of population and vehicles not so unlike Manhattan, after all.

Then there's the matter of not knowing where she is. I buy

some biscuits, just in case we see her. I think maybe I glimpse her down a block, in the afternoon, but it's too far away to be certain, and then the yellowy-ochre shape is gone.

But I am not really looking, because I understand that this time I cannot help. And that something has happened, she's brought me something: that encounter, on the sidewalk, that dear, needy paw extended to my hand, that surrender of weight—it has opened my heart. I understand that it is a cliché to say so, but how else to describe it? We lock the gates of the self against pain; it is inevitable that we should come to do so, for who can live without protection in the world of time? A saint, I suppose. A bleeding Cristo. For the rest of us, the wounds of loss, the nicks and cuts made by our own sense of powerlessness, must form a sort of carapace, an armor.

But what I learn, that night on Calle Canal, and afterward, sleeping fitfully in our room, and the next day, packing up, walking the streets to buy some gifts for friends, shipping a box of our purchases home, is that my armor has changed.

Once, having built myself a carapace against despair, I sank under the weight of that protective encasement. But that shield has been slowly falling away. What I feel for this naked creature on the streets of San Miguel isn't despair. It's compassion, pure and simple, grief for her situation, sorrow for her lot. Feeling this makes me more alive, not less so. It doesn't make me feel hopeless.

Why not? Of course her prospects aren't good, and it cuts to the quick that I can't come to her assistance when she asks for help with such grace and dignity. Even so, she is able to ask for help. I am able to stand with her and feel a pang of longing, and carry that sorrow with me, and still not feel the world is a hopeless place. She and I are both vulnerable, equally subject to the predations of illness and of time. I have my privileged resources, but they only protect me to a point; the animal self is always subject to destruction, no matter what. She might come to a better end; the brief extension of my hand to her might have made some little difference.

I accidentally leave the bag of biscuits I've bought in the Pak-Mail shop. I come home to the elderly, grateful, slightly ridiculous creature who has depended upon me for years. I understand that I have turned some corner now, that I am willing; that I will not harm myself; that I have work to do in the world; that I am grateful to have felt even this sharp sadness. That to give one's attention to the image of a suffering Christ is to make it clear that one is not afraid of pain. Despair is one note in the range of feeling that will pour through me, over time, but I do not have to be frozen there, locked in that absence of futurity and of hope. Animal presences remain for me, as they have always been, a door toward feeling and understanding. The dog on Calle Canal awakens me; she shows me that I have come through something now. I write to bless her delicate head, the paw raised in hope. How should we know ourselves, except in the clarifying mirror of some other gaze?

Second Wind

*S*tanley Kunitz says someplace that if poetry teaches us anything at all, it is that we can believe two apparently contradictory things at once. Emily Dickinson is the great teacher of contradiction. She understands that no single position tells the truth, that the representation of human experience requires contradiction, polarity, the free movement between opposing points of view.

And thus she gives us, after the terrifying wind that blew not from the orchard but from some far source of devastation and erasure, a gust of entirely different air.

Of all the Sounds dispatched abroad—
There's not a charge to me
Like that old measure in the Boughs
That phraseless Melody—
The Wind does—working like a Hand
Whose fingers brush the Sky—
Then quiver down—with Tufts of Tune—
Permitted men—and me—

Inheritance it is—to us
Beyond the Art to earn—

Beyond the trait to take away—
By Robber—since the Gain
Is gotten, not with fingers—
And inner than the Bone—
Hid golden—for the whole of Days—

This wind is the music of the world, entering us, and though it's
"phraseless"—a music without measure—it quivers down to us, it
comes in bits of melody. It's our inheritance from the world, that sound.
Like poetry itself, such music seems a gift, one you can't quite earn nor
have stolen from you, since it has no materiality. The "Gain" of music
or poetry becomes, once really heard, an internal possession, something
that is, in a beautifully eccentric phrase, "inner than the Bone."
    And because such music—the internalized cadence—becomes part
of us, Dickinson goes on to a startling speculation:

And even in the Urn—
I cannot vouch the merry Dust
Do not arise and play—
In some odd fashion of it's own—
Some quainter Holiday—
When Winds go round and round, in Bands—
And thrum upon the Door—
And Birds take places—Overhead—
To bear them Orchestra—

Surely that is a speculation that, were he granted by nature the abil-
ity to understand poetry, Mr. Beau's spirit would approve of: that the
joyous wind of the world could stir even the remnant ashes of the body to
play, that even in death the music of things might fill us with delight.

In this vision of things, one is not, emphatically, a "fool to stay"—
or even to leave, since joy is so much a characteristic of the world's
operations that it follows us even into the Urn.

Dickinson wants to make sure that all the living hear the air with
her, and so her poem concludes

I crave him grace—of Summer Boughs—
If such an Outcast be—
He never heard that fleshless Chant
Rise solemn, in the Tree—
As if some Caravan of sound
On Deserts, in the Sky
Had broken Rank—
Then knit—and passed—
in Seamless Company—

Fleshless, descended from the sky, the wind comes, breaking away
from whatever sky-crossing caravan it once belonged to, then rising and
joining again. That, at least in this poem's terms, is what we also do:
join a seamless company, held in the music that is the world's delight-
ing motion.

The question is, that wind that I heard blowing through the bed into
the ether beyond it when Wally died, the wind that blew Beau into
whatever it was that came next—was that the wind of contingency
and disruption, or could it have been the wind of joy?

Are we certain, Miss Dickinson, dear teacher speaking from
Amherst one hundred and forty years ago, as clear and confounding as
if you wrote these words this morning—are we sure that these are two
different winds?

Chapter Sixteen

The old man who lived on my block in Provincetown devised a method to help his ancient springer spaniel walk, when the dog became too old and weak to lift himself up. Antony made a rope harness that he'd slip around Charlie's torso, and he'd haul the old sad sack up, a few inches off the ground, and then the dog could move his legs on his own, and together they'd go for a walk.

This always seemed to me a synthesis of love and art; craft found a way, for a while, to keep the beloved other in the world.

⟫⟪

Love and art—those two towers can't be knocked down, can they? Though you can, for a stretch of time, lose sight of them.

⟫⟪

Wherever Arden's anxiety came from, it faded as mysteriously as it had come; where he had seemed distracted and out of focus, his clear, direct gaze was restored, that curious brown look—filmed by age but still imminently recognizable: curiosity, a readiness for enjoyment, an interest in seeing what comes next. I'll catalog his late-life pleasures, alphabetically:

Going to the BEACH. Unable, now, to walk down to the water, or do his old fling-yourself-on-the-sand-and-roll routine, but able to hobble from the parking lot over to the edge of dune and lie down at the first spot where he could see the water. Then, pleased as any living thing might be, sit with the wind in his ears, sniffing, observant.

BISCUITS.

Riding in the CAR. He knows when we're packing for a trip, even a little one, and begins to snort and express excitement. It's hard for him to wait till we're ready; he'd prefer to be bundled into the car first, and sit in the back, happy and panting on his blanket while we load everything else. That way, it's clear he's the most important item to be brought along.

DEMONSTRATING, through a nonstop, willful exertion, the figure of determination, that he can still climb the three flights of stairs to our apartment.

There are a number of FRIENDS who visit Arden and help us out, in these late years. Genine, who comes to visit in our longest days at work, when Arden has to be by himself for hours, and sketches portraits of him, and invites him to go out for a walk, though he usually refuses. Sarah, a poet from my class at NYU, stays with Arden while we're in London, to the complete happiness of all parties involved. And the person he comes to love best, Kathy, a poet and teacher who seems to have precisely the right energy for old dogs, who seems to be on his wavelength. I am at a loss to explain this, exactly, but then why should the particular sympathy between any two creatures lend itself to explication? Though the bond between them sparks one to try. Paul is convinced that it's because Kathy is from Wildwood, New Jersey, a honky-tonk strip of motels, boardwalk, and amusement park along the shore, and that she thus carries something of one of Arden's favorite places, those New Jersey beaches, about her very person. Paul's fascination with his native state is so intense that it has perhaps resulted in just a *bit* of projection. My sense is that she has all the qualities Arden likes: she is affectionate but not overly attentive, down-to-earth, and likes to read in bed with him. She is confident, unfussy, and enjoys having a routine. Arden's quite adaptable, having been a country dog and a city one, having shied away from small-town crowds and then taken pleasure in urban scenes—but he likes to establish a pattern that we'll repeat for a while, at least; that's one of his pleasures, too, knowing what to do next, because we did this same thing yesterday. In this way, he's come to know the path to the Cuban coffee shop in Key West, the stores in Provincetown that offer biscuits to passing canines. In this way, Arden's very like me—he likes having a routine, and then he likes for that routine to change, in order to keep things interesting. (*Now* who's projecting!) Kathy has herself lost an old father, not so long ago, as well as an old dog of her own; she seems to understand something about physical limitation, and about keeping company. I don't know what it is, but after they've been together, Arden is completely, unmistakably fine; I may have been off running around, worrying about him in between engagements, but I step through the apartment door, and he's placid and at ease, having been perfectly comfortable in the company of his friend.

Exercising entire HEGEMONY over a motel bed of his own.

Paul's parents' summerhouse, a little place on the JERSEY SHORE. There's a chain-link fence around the backyard (a detail I include here to Paul's regret; even as children, he and his brothers lobbied their parents for some more attractive boundary) and, just beyond that, a small dock and a lagoon. Occasionally, a boat goes by, but mostly what passes are egrets and seagulls, herons and time. Arden is content to lie all day in the grass beside the detested fence, watching the lagoon, moving into the shade awhile if the sun's too hot, then back to watch the water some more. In fact, every time we drive through the Holland Tunnel and make our way south of the refineries, he *does* seem delighted by New Jersey. And then, at the exit on the Garden State Parkway for Somers Point, he lumbers out of his rest, head to the glass, sniffing the salt air, brimming with anticipation.

OCCUPYING a great deal of space in our bed—lying on his side, all four legs stretched straight out, so that we must fit ourselves in around the edges and, when we have had enough, gently but firmly fold him up.

＝＝

His PAUL—that's how we put it, *Arden loves his Paul*. I am pulled away often on business of one sort or another, making a living, but Paul has a steadier schedule, and Arden's learned to count on him being around, and loves nothing better than to give him one of the demonstrations of affection he likes best, what we think of as Arden's version of a hug: he buries his face in your chest, as you kneel in front of him, and pushes the top of his head against you, as if to express your love for someone is to disappear into them as far as you can go. Beau's notion was different: he liked to push his hindquarters against you, so that you'd scratch above his tail, while he delightedly looked outward at the world. Arden thinks love is expressed by focusing solely on the object of your affection.

＝＝

Going out to the SIDEWALK in Manhattan, letting the life of the street swirl around him. Two years ago, we'd walk to the bakery on Eighteenth Street, for coffee and a shared muffin. Last year, we'd walk around the block. Then, just to the corner, and now, we go, really, nowhere—out to the sidewalk. Arden lies down and waits to see what will take place. His best friends on the street, like him, are slow on their feet, unsteady in the hips. They say, "How's he doing?" I say, "A little slow today." And, invariably, they'll laugh and say, "Oh, me too." They beam at him with unguarded affection.

SLEEPING in the garden, in Provincetown, under the shade of a sprawling Montauk daisy, no matter how hot the day. At night, too, I'll hear him push the sliding screen door in the kitchen open with his muzzle—he long ago made a hole in the bottom, expressly for this purpose—and then he'll wobble his way out to that same spot, and lie in the cool darkness under leaves and stars.

A TOWEL DRY, given after going outside in the rain; marvelous, being rubbed all over with a slightly rough cloth.

TRIUMPH, his favorite food, reliably delicious; he has never been known not to finish a bowl.

WATCHING a mouse on the floor of our apartment, one who'd crept out to look at him, and sat staring up at the dark giant who has no intention whatsoever of doing anything about its presence, who is merely interested.

Drugs for Arden, part two:

Glucosamine, a daily supplement to keep the joints working. Does it help? I never know, though, once commenced, it seems a bad idea to stop it.

Rimadyl, an anti-inflammatory, enables those tender old joints to flex, and it works for Arden for many months, a long time, allowing a leg to lift, creaky hips and thighs to get to poise in that necessary retriever squat.

Enalapril, heart pills. For a while now, he's had a cough, and we learn from Dr. Kaiser, his gentle Provincetown vet, that the congestion's caused by the arrhythmia Tandy Tupper noticed years ago. (Funny to think she thought him on the brink of the grave back when he was ten—which would be, if you believe that one dog year equals seven human ones, forty-two years ago.)

Adequan, an injected drug first used for horses with joint problems caused by running, powerful stuff that could cause cartilage to regenerate. Dr. Kaiser gives him just a few shots, one a week, and it works awhile, until it doesn't.

Deramaxx, another generation of Rimadyl, a bit better, and once again, the stuff keeps an old boy moving longer than he could on his own.

First, he falls on a few stairs on the way down to the street, missing his footing. The lightbulb's burnt out on the landing, and he seems furious about it, trying to find the step; perhaps, to his dimmed eyes, that dim hallway's really just darkness. Then, a few days later, even with new bulbs illuminating the way, he stumbles going up, and actually tumbles down nearly a whole flight to the landing, scaring Paul half to death. Happily, Arden seems partly made of rubber, his limbs twisting akimbo without any apparent harm. But the day comes when the stairs to the apartment are impossible; that old right hind leg just seems a delicate, withering thing, and there's simply no way he can manage. We carry him, but it's ridiculous to try to lug him up and down every time he needs to go out, even when I remember to keep my knees bent. And it's doubtless awful for him, one of us trying to lug seventy-five pounds of dog up and down the stairs every time he needs to go out. He *does* feel lighter now, in the way that old men get stringier and less meaty, but there's still a lot of him.

Luckily, it's a semester when we're off work, more or less. We have freedom to move, and can take Arden up to the house in Provincetown much earlier than we'd usually go to our summer place. We arrive in April, when it's leaden and chill, and the house seems glad to see us, suddenly lit with lamps and fires and habitation. To be there is a huge, immediate relief: Arden can live on one floor and spend as much time outside as he likes. We don't have to worry about getting him quickly in and out, and if he doesn't make it outside one day, it's not a problem—these old wood floors have already seen two hundred years of action, and nothing's going to hurt them. Plus he's known this house forever. It's a fine, easy place to be old.

And, so, six weeks pass, as the calendar moves toward Arden's sixteenth birthday, sometime in April, then on into May.

Dr. Kaiser is gentle with Arden, and wouldn't dream of doing anything invasive. I like him; he's soft-spoken, curious about the creature before him. Though he is physically large, he does not seem to think of himself as such—the way Newfoundlands, say, seem vaguely apologetic for their size, a bit of slow delicacy in their largeness. Dr. Kaiser thinks it's great that Arden's had such a long span on earth, and he knows how attached to him we are. He makes no unrealistic attempts or promises or offers at all. Now it's all about comfort; he understands that, at this point, whatever life is left to this old survivor is, as they say, gravy.

Arden, naturally, does not like Dr. Kaiser as much as I do. He puts up with him, though, and cautiously accepts the liver-flavored vitamins the vet holds out to him.

Now the nickname that Paul has always favored for Arden seems the best: Tiny. Brave fellow, huffing along, figuring out how to move that uncooperative body from spot to spot. "Where is that Tiny," we say. Napping under the budding forsythia, out on the gravel staring at sparrows. Although we sleep upstairs, Arden soon abandons any notion of coming up with us: he's happy to stay downstairs on the living-room rug, or, if we've built a fire that evening, on the bare floor of the dining room, where it's cooler. As spring comes on, he's more and more in the garden, staying in one place for long stretches. We have some little outings: trips to the vet, followed by a drive to the beach. The last time we go, he's clearly too sore and tired to even get out of the car, but we leave the tailgate open so he can look out and breathe in that current of Atlantic air.

And then he's in the kitchen all the time, where his food and water are, on the cool quarry-tile floor. People always said to me, *You'll know when it's time,* and I never believed it—not with this dog, who wanted so much to stay in the world. I was terrified that his body would fail him, would refuse to go another step, an awful sprawl beneath him, and he'd be looking at me in a confusion and panic, just wanting to live.

Dr. Kaiser says, "Call me any time, I'll come to the house. You'll know when it's time."

Arden seems nervous, his breathing's hard. In pain, I think. The

Triumph goes unfinished. He falls, and I try to reach beneath him and lift up those crumpled hindquarters, and he cries out terribly.

There's a Friday morning when I wake up and hear him crying before I've even walked into the kitchen, and there he is, sprawled on the floor in a puddle of urine and feces he's been trying to drag himself out of, completely helpless. And the look on his face— well, I know what it means, beyond any doubt.

I clean him up and call Dr. Kaiser, who understands the situation but can't come till Sunday. Certainly, it's better for us that we have a little time. I think it'll be all right; we can take care of him. What I'd imagined I wouldn't be able to stand was the feeling that Arden would still want to live, that he'd have every intention of going on no matter how helpless his body: hell on earth. But that isn't the case; what was entirely plain to me in his face that morning was that he was through, that he'd welcome an exit.

Once I've made the call, Arden seems to lighten, to change, as if he knows the path is clear. He still can't move, but he seems at ease, distraction giving way to that old, clear gaze, his tension evaporating. It's as if there's an element of relief for Paul and me, what we've so long known was coming here at last, and Arden must feel it, too.

And now we give him the warmest and lightest weekend we can. He seems to relax utterly. We spend time brushing and stroking him. We cuddle him up and talk. He sleeps in the garden, his last night, in the cool air under the stars, and Sunday morning has grilled chicken for breakfast, and he's sprawled sleepily on the gravel by the gate when Dr. Kaiser comes. My sense, for whatever it's worth, is that he knows perfectly well where we've arrived. Does he give one little growl at the vet, as if for old times' sake? As if it were his duty, and he'd be some other dog if he didn't?

This is unmitigatedly awful and not so at all; I remind myself this is exactly what I'd want, for someone to love me enough not to allow me to live in pain when I don't want to; that it's part of our work—this is what Dr. Kaiser has said to us—part of our stewardship, seeing Arden out of the world.

I have my face down against that smooth muzzle, the ears that still smell, as they have all his life, of corn muffins. Paul's holding him from the other side, so that we can both be in his gaze. We each speak to him quietly. First, there's a shot to relax him, to make sure the second shot will work, and I don't think he even feels it. And then we ease him out of that worn-out body with a kiss, and he's gone like a whisper, the easiest breath.

We'd long planned to bury him in the garden, near where Beau lies, in his favorite spot under the forsythia. But when it came to it, truly we couldn't do it. Wasn't Arden a dog who always really just wanted to be with us anyway? Leave it to Beau for commingling with all things wild; Arden preferred his human company. So, we let the vet take his body to be cremated, down Cape someplace, his ashes to be returned in a few days. Dr. Kaiser lifts him—still a serious bulk, though he looks so light now—and then, oh! what empties out my heart all over again, how his neck lolls like a loose flower on a stem. Just like Wally's; how, after months and months of rigidity, the gradual paralysis afflicting his nervous system and muscles pulling his head tightly to one side—and then, suddenly, in death, that tightness released as if it had never been there. Who

knew that Arden had been holding his neck with all that tension?
He'd worked so hard, old soldier, to hold himself upright, to will
his uncooperating hips to the next step, the next position. I'm
remembering the tension in his shoulders, the way those muscles
worked overtime, to compensate. And now, all effort released, the
neck just floats.

The vet sets his sweet body in the back of the black pickup
truck. I can't help it, I have to rearrange his head and neck so he
looks comfortable, even though I know it's absurd. The vet
understands my gesture, and we thank him for all he's done for
us, and then he drives away.

We try our best. *A good end,* we tell ourselves, *a fine end, the best
we could do.* We talk about Mr. Arden and the stories of his days,
and then we don't, for a while, and we each allow ourselves to
weep—usually one at a time, because somehow doing it together
just seems too much for us to take. *A long life,* we say, *a fine life,
and not nearly enough.*

Sometimes the house is so empty we can hardly bear it, and then
sometimes it seems like no one's gone—isn't Arden in one of his
favored spots, watching us? Won't he, in a moment, come around
the door? He's an absence and a presence both—the way he will
be, to greater or lesser degrees, for years to come.

We keep collecting his hair in its little dark puffs from the
floor.

Paul finds an empty can of Triumph in the recycling bin, and
we put the hair in there, on the mantel.

We make a memorial ad, as people in our small town like to do,

to tell the community about the passing of loved dogs, and take it
down to the newspaper office. The fellow who takes our ad has an
old dog, too. We bring a photo of Arden on the beach, and his
name and dates, and a stanza from the most unabashed elegy for a
dog I know, Robinson Jeffers's "The Housedog's Grave," in
which an English bulldog named Haig speaks from his grave, outside the window of the house where he'd lived:

> I've changed my ways a little, I cannot now
> Run with you in the evenings along the shore,
> Except in a kind of dream, and you, if you dream a moment,
> You see me there.

Wouldn't you know that the most misanthropic of poets would
write the warmest of elegies for his dog? I e-mail the poem to
people who've known Arden, to tell them he's gone. I cut out the
last words, and put them on the table where I write, next to a photograph of Arden in the deep green of the summer garden: *I am
not lonely. I am not afraid. I am still yours.*

They help a bit, those lines.

Paul and I are strangely unanchored. We take ourselves out for
strolls to the bay, go across town to look at the marsh, amble back,
noticing the gardens and the new shops. We stop for coffee. We sit
a long time, on the bench in front of the coffee bar. No hurry. This
feels strange to me, unfamiliar. For sixteen years, there has been
someone at home, waiting to go for a walk.

Envoi

Toy Wolf

For Christmas, one of the things I give Paul is sponsorship of a wolf cub in Yellowstone or Alaska, one of those programs run by an organization for wildlife; for a small donation, he gets the pleasure of knowing he might be helping a creature to thrive.

I figure he'll get a certificate or a card, and I've more or less forgotten about it, in December, when a padded envelope arrives. I give it to him to open, and inside's a stuffed, not unreasonably cute little wolf. When you squeeze it, the toy lets out a poignant, quite effective mechanical howl, the sort of thing that both tugs at your emotions a bit and makes you laugh, all at once.

I figure this is a gift I'll never see again. But sure enough, in a while, I notice it's sitting on Paul's nightstand. Then, one day, it's in the bed, I discover, when I roll over and it lets loose that plaintive yowl.

I'm not sure which of us does it first, but soon the cub is positioned up near the pillows, when one of us makes the bed, and the next thing you know, he's recumbent in some bedding made from a T-shirt or a scarf. We're making a space for him.

We aren't ready for another dog quite yet—Arden's and Beau's are big pawprints to fill, and we've had years and years of elderly pets, and there's so much travel in our lives just now, so the time hasn't felt right.

But now and then, one of us will go into the bedroom for something, and then the other will be startled by that funny little cry.